Full-Size Bed Quilts

LEISURE ARTS®

CREATED FOR LEISURE ARTS BY HOUSE OF WHITE BIRCHES

Contents

FULL-SIZE BED QUILTS ©2003, 2001, 2000, 1999, 1998, 1997 House of White Birches, 306 East Parr Road, Berne, IN 46711, (260) 589-4000. Customer_Service@ whitebirches.com. Made in USA.

ISBN: 1-57486-358-4

Introduction

The first choice of many quilters is making full-size quilts. It's been this way from the beginning, with diligent and caring women making quilts as bedcovers and blankets for their families. Although the use remains the same, creative women now find dozens of reasons to make a quilt.

English Wedding Ring

Exotic Petals

Special occasions and holidays are perfect times to stitch up brand-new quilts. The English Wedding Ring on page 18 was designed to celebrate an anniversary with plain squares providing space for the wedding guests to sign. Circle of Friendship on page 98 honors both patriotism and friendship in a clever design made by separating the red-and-white blocks with blue sashing strips.

Full-size quilts are excellent for raffles. Exotic Petals on page 52 was designed for that purpose by a quilt guild in Indiana. Trailing Blossoms on page 111 is the result of a group of quilters having a block exchange. This is a quick way to make a full-size quilt because everyone in the group contributes a block.

Warm and fuzzy flannel is a favorite quilt fabric, inviting all to snuggle up on chilly nights. A Fondness for Flannel and Falling Stars are made with large patchwork pieces that can be stitched together in a relatively short time. Have you tried a tessellating design? You'll want to create the interesting Two-Part Harmony quilt. It looks complicated but is really fairly easy to construct.

Intriguing color patterns and geometric designs fascinate quilters and nonquilters alike, making for hours of interesting study and conversation. Large quilts give you the opportunity to create a variety of glorious designs. As many quilters will tell you, "I never met a full-size quilt I didn't like!" ❖

Trailing Blossoms

Broken Trails

BY JOLYN OLSON

Although this quilt is called Broken Trails, it actually contains two blocks, Broken Trails and Snowball. Broken Trails might add the pattern, but the Snowball block leaves lots of open space for creative quilting. With the quick-piecing methods given here, the quilt can be completed in record time, which will leave plenty of time and space to permit the quilter to show off her hand- or machine-quilting skills.

Broken Trails

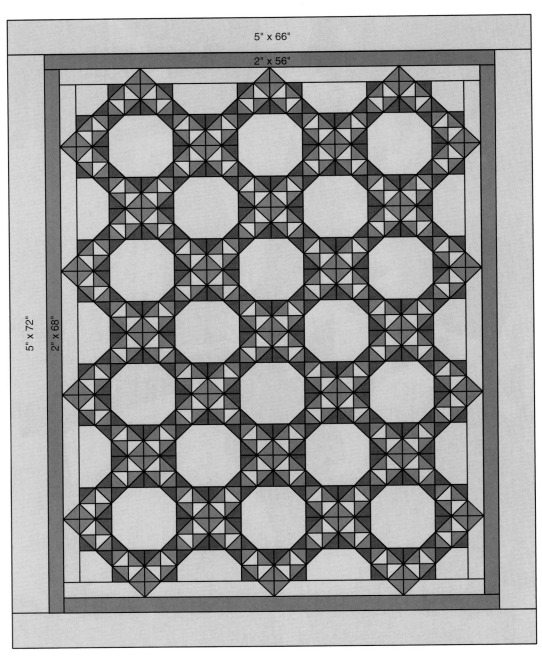

5" x 66"

2" x 56"

5" x 72"

2" x 68"

Broken Trails
Placement Diagram
66" x 82"

Broken Trails

Project Specifications

Quilt Size: 66" x 82"

Block Size: 8" x 8"

Number of Blocks: 17 Broken Trail blocks; 18 Snowball blocks and 14 half-blocks

Fabric & Batting

- 1¼ yards burgundy print
- 2 yards black print
- 4 yards gray check
- Backing 70" x 86"
- Batting 70" x 86"
- 8½ yards self-made or purchased binding

Supplies & Tools

- Neutral color and white all-purpose thread
- Basic sewing tools and supplies, rotary cutter, mat and ruler

Instructions

1. Cut 14 strips black print 2⅞" by fabric width; subcut into 2⅞" square segments. Cut each square in half on one diagonal to make A triangles; you will need 384 black print A triangles.

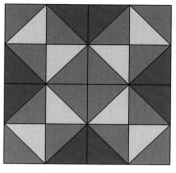

Broken Trail
8" x 8" Block

Snowball
8" x 8" Block

2. Cut two strips black print 2½" by fabric width; subcut into 2½" segments to make B squares. You will need 28 black print B squares.

3. Cut seven strips burgundy print 2⅞" by fabric width; subcut into 2⅞" square segments. Cut each square in half on one diagonal to make A triangles; you will need 192 burgundy print A triangles.

4. Cut seven strips burgundy print 2½" by fabric width; subcut into 2½" segments to make B squares. You will need 96 burgundy print B squares.

5. Cut seven strips gray check 2⅞" by fabric width; subcut into 2⅞" square segments. Cut each square in half on one diagonal to make A triangles; you will need 192 gray check A triangles.

Broken Trails

6. Cut three strips gray check 4½" by fabric width; subcut into four 4½" segments for D squares and ten 8½" segments for E rectangles.

7. Cut seven strips gray check 2½" by fabric width; subcut into ten 16½" segments for H, four 10½" segments for G and four 8½" segments for F.

8. Cut five strips gray check 8½" by fabric width; subcut into eighteen 8½" segments to make C squares.

9. To piece one Broken Trail block, join a gray check A triangle with a black print A triangle to make a triangle/square A unit as shown in Figure 1; repeat for eight gray/black A units.

Figure 1
Join a gray check A triangle with a
black print A triangle to make a
gray/black A unit.

10. Join a black print A triangle with a burgundy print A triangle to make a triangle/square A unit as shown in Figure 2; repeat for eight burgundy/black A units.

Figure 2
Join a black print A triangle with a
burgundy print A triangle to make
a burgundy/black A unit.

11. Join two gray/black A units with two burgundy/black A units to make a block as shown in Figure 3; repeat for four block units.

Figure 3
Join A units to
make a block unit.

12. Join four block units to complete one Broken Trail block as shown in Figure 4; repeat for 17 blocks.

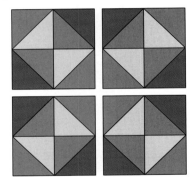

Figure 4
Join 4 block units to complete
1 Broken Trail block.

13. Repeat steps 9–11 to make two block units. Join two block units to complete a half-block as shown in Figure 5; repeat for 14 half-blocks.

Figure 5
Join 2 block units to
complete a half-block.

14. To piece one Snowball block, sew a burgundy print B square to each corner of a gray check C square as shown in Figure 6. Trim seam allowance to ¼" beyond seams; press remaining triangles flat to complete one Snowball block as shown in Figure 7. Repeat for 18 blocks.

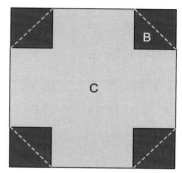

Figure 6
Sew a burgundy print B
square to each corner of
a gray check C square.

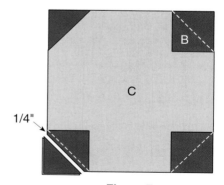

Figure 7
Trim seam allowance to 1/4"
beyond seams; press
remaining triangle flat to
create 1 Snowball block.

15. Sew a burgundy print B square to one corner of a D square as in step 14; trim and press to make a corner square as shown in Figure 8. Repeat for four corner squares.

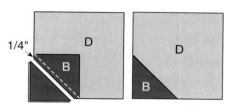

Figure 8
Trim and press to make
a corner square.

16. Sew a burgundy print square to two corners of an E rectangle as shown in Figure 9. Trim and press to make E rectangle units; repeat for 10 rectangle units.

Figure 9
Sew a burgundy print B
square to 2 corners of a
gray check E rectangle.

Broken Trails

17. Join two corner squares, three half-blocks and two E rectangle units to make a row as shown in Figure 10; repeat for two rows; press.

Figure 10
Join 2 corner squares, 3 half-blocks and
2 E rectangle units to make a row.

18. Join two E rectangle units, three Broken Trail blocks and two Snowball blocks to make a row as shown in Figure 11; repeat for three rows.

Figure 11
Join 2 E rectangle units, 3 Broken Trail blocks
and 2 Snowball blocks to make a row.

19. Join two half-blocks, three Snowball blocks and two Broken Trail blocks to make a row as shown in Figure 12; repeat for four rows.

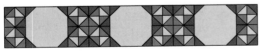

Figure 12
Join 2 half-blocks, 3 Snowball blocks
and 2 Broken Trail blocks to make a row.

20. Arrange the rows referring to Figure 13; join rows to complete pieced center.

Figure 13
Arrange the rows as shown.

21. Sew a black print B square to one end of an F rectangle as in step 14 and referring to Figure 14; repeat for four B-F units.

Figure 14
Sew a black print B square to 1 end of F.

22. Sew a black print B square to each end of a G rectangle as in step 14 and referring to Figure 15; repeat for four B-G units.

Figure 15
Sew a black print B square to 1 end of G.

23. Sew a black print B square to each end of an H rectangle as in step 14 and referring to Figure 16; repeat for 10 B-H units.

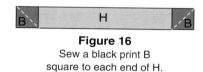

Figure 16
Sew a black print B
square to each end of H.

24. Join three B-H units with two B-F units to make a strip as shown in Figure 17; repeat for two strips. Sew a strip to opposite long sides of the pieced center; press seams toward strips.

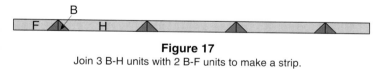

Figure 17
Join 3 B-H units with 2 B-F units to make a strip.

25. Join two B-H units with two B-G units to make a strip as shown in Figure 18; repeat for two strips. Sew a strip to the top and bottom of the pieced center; press seams toward strips.

Figure 18
Join 2 B-H units with 2 B-G units to make a strip.

26. Cut and piece two strips each black print 2½" x 56½" and 2½" x 68½". Sew the longer strips to opposite long sides and the shorter strips to the top and bottom; press seams toward strips.

27. Cut and piece two strips each gray check 5½" x 66½" and 5½" x 72½". Sew the longer strips to opposite long sides and the shorter strips to the top and bottom; press seams toward strips.

28. Sandwich batting between completed top and prepared backing piece. Pin or baste layers together to hold flat.

29. Quilt as desired by hand or machine. *Note: The quilt shown was machine-quilted using white quilting thread and a purchased quilting design in the Snowball block centers and on the borders. When quilting is complete, remove pins or basting; trim edges even.*

30. Bind edges with self-made or purchased binding to finish. ❖

Silver Linings

BY LUCY A. FAZELY

Blue skies always have a silver lining, and this quilt created with many blue fabrics displays its silver lining through the triangles of shimmering metallic prints that the designer has added. If you can't find metallic prints, try other fabrics of a similar hue that will enhance the blue.

Silver Linings

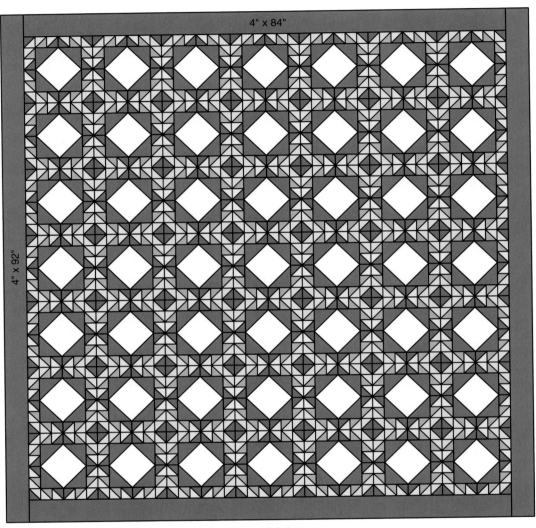

4" x 84"

4" x 92"

Silver Linings
Placement Diagram
92" x 92"

Silver Linings

Project Specifications

Quilt Size: 92" x 92"

Block Size: 12" x 12"

Number of Blocks: 49

Fabric & Batting

- 1½ yards medium blue floral
- 1½ yards silver/gold print
- 1⅔ yards light blue floral
- 2 yards silver/blue print
- 4¾ yards dark blue print
- Backing 96" x 96"
- Batting 96" x 96"
- 10¾ yards self-made or purchased binding

Supplies & Tools

- Neutral color all-purpose thread
- Basic sewing tools and supplies, rotary cutter, mat and ruler

Instructions

1. Prepare templates using pattern pieces given; cut as directed on each piece for one block. Repeat for 49 blocks.

2. To piece one block, sew B to each side of A; press seams toward B.

Silver Linings
12" x 12" Block

3. Sew a dark blue print C to a silver/gold print C as shown in Figure 1 to make C1; repeat for eight C1 units. Sew a silver/blue print C to a medium blue floral C to make C2; repeat for eight C2 units. Sew a dark blue print C to a silver/blue print C to make C3; repeat for four C3 units.

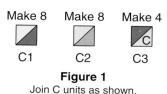

Make 8   Make 8   Make 4

C1   C2   C3

Figure 1
Join C units as shown.

4. Join a C1 and C2 unit as shown in Figure 2; repeat for eight C1-C2 units. Join two units as shown in Figure 3. Repeat for four units. Sew a unit to opposite sides of the A-B unit as shown in Figure 4.

Make 4   Make 4

C2 C1   C1 C2

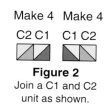

Figure 2
Join a C1 and C2 unit as shown.

Figure 3
Join 2 units as shown.

Figure 4
Sew a unit to opposite sides of the A-B unit.

Silver Linings

5. Sew a C3 unit to each end of the remaining pieced units as shown in Figure 5; sew these units to the remaining sides of the A-B-C unit to complete one block. Repeat for 49 blocks.

Figure 5
Sew a C3 unit to each end of the remaining pieced units as shown.

6. Lay out blocks in seven rows of seven blocks each; join blocks in rows. Join rows to complete the pieced center; press seams in one direction.

7. Cut and piece two strips each 4½" x 84½" and 4½" x 92½" dark blue print. Sew the shorter strips to the top and bottom and longer strips to opposite sides. Press seams toward strips.

8. Sandwich batting between completed top and prepared backing piece; pin or baste layers together to hold flat.

9. Quilt as desired by hand or machine.

10. When quilting is complete, trim edges even and remove pins or basting.

11. Bind edges with self-made or purchased binding to finish. ❖

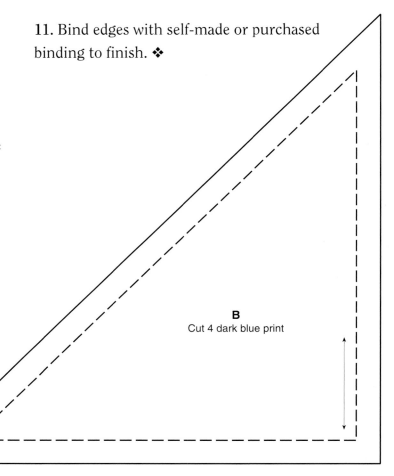

B
Cut 4 dark blue print

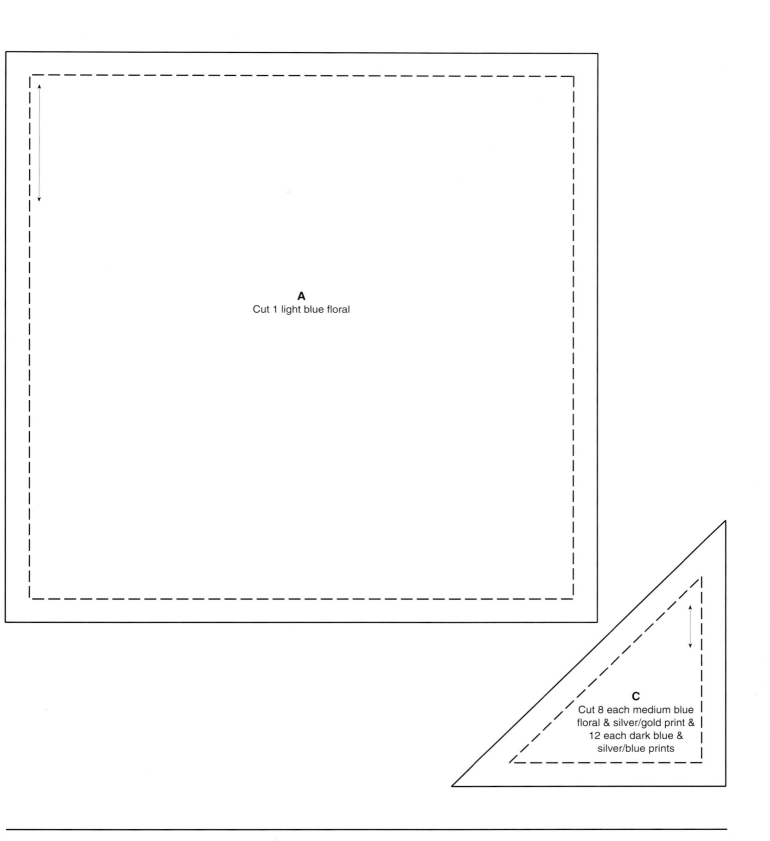

A
Cut 1 light blue floral

C
Cut 8 each medium blue
floral & silver/gold print &
12 each dark blue &
silver/blue prints

English Wedding Ring

BY JILL REBER

This quilt was originally created by the designer to celebrate her 20th wedding anniversary. It's a beautiful quilt to make as an anniversary or wedding gift. The many plain squares provide space for the wedding guests to sign, leaving a permanent memento of a glorious occasion.

English Wedding Ring

English Wedding Ring
Placement Diagram
65" x 85"

English Wedding Ring

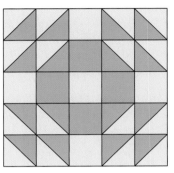

English Wedding Ring
10" x 10" Block

Project Specifications

Quilt Size: 65" x 85"

Block Size: 10" x 10"

Number of Blocks: 18

Fabric & Batting

- 18 strips various coordinating prints 6" x 44"
- 1½ yards large floral print
- 4 yards beige-on-beige print
- Backing 69" x 89"
- Batting 69" x 89"
- 9 yards self-made or purchased binding

Supplies & Tools

- All-purpose thread to match fabrics
- Basic sewing supplies and tools, rotary cutter, mat and ruler

Instructions

1. Cut eight 2⅞" squares from each one of each of the 6" x 44" print strips. Cut each square in half on one diagonal to make 16 triangles from each print. Cut a 2½" x 12" rectangle from the remainder of each strip.

2. Cut 11 strips beige-on-beige print 2⅞" by fabric width. Cut 144 squares 2⅞" from strips; cut each square on one diagonal to make 288 triangles.

3. Cut seven strips 2½" by fabric width beige-on-beige print. Subcut into eighteen 2½" x 12" rectangles. Cut the remaining pieces into 18 squares 2½" x 2½".

4. Sew a print triangle to a beige-on-beige triangle to make a triangle/square; repeat for all triangles, making 16 triangle/squares for each block.

English Wedding Ring

5. Sew a 2½" x 12" print rectangle to a 2½" x 12" beige-on-beige rectangle. Press seams toward print fabric. Repeat for all print rectangles. Cut each stitched set into four 2½" segments as shown in Figure 1.

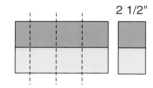

Figure 1
Cut stitched strips into 2 1/2" segments.

6. Join four same-fabric triangle/square units as shown in Figure 2; repeat for four units. Join the triangle/square units with the units cut in step 5 and a 2½" x 2½" beige-on-beige square as shown in Figure 3 to complete one block. Repeat for 18 blocks. Square up blocks to 10½" x 10½", if necessary.

Figure 2
Join 4 same-fabric
triangle/squares as shown.

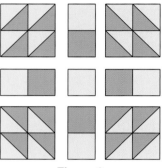

Figure 3
Join units to make a block as shown.

7. Cut five strips beige-on-beige print 10½" by fabric width. Cut each strip into four 10½" units. Repeat for 17 squares.

8. Join three pieced blocks with two beige-on-beige print blocks to make a row as shown in Figure 4; repeat for four rows. Press seams in one direction.

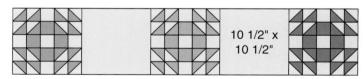

Figure 4
Join 3 pieced blocks with 2 print blocks to make a row.

9. Join two pieced blocks with three beige-on-beige print blocks to make a row as shown in Figure 5; repeat for three rows. Press seams in the opposite direction from previous rows.

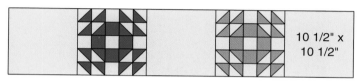

Figure 5
Join 2 pieced blocks with 3 print blocks to make a row.

10. Referring to the Placement Diagram, join rows, beginning and ending with a three-block row; press seams in one direction.

11. Cut two strips beige-on-beige print 2½" x 50½". Sew a strip to the top and bottom of the pieced center; press seams toward strips.

12. Cut two more strips beige-on-beige print 2½" x 74½". Sew a strip to opposite long sides; press seams toward strips.

13. Cut two strips large floral print 6" x 54½". Sew a strip to the top and bottom of the pieced center; press seams toward strips.

14. Cut two more strips large floral print 6" x 85½". Sew a strip to opposite long sides of the pieced center; press seams toward strips.

15. Mark a pretty quilting design in the print blocks using a water-erasable marker or pencil.

16. Sandwich batting between completed top and prepared backing piece. Pin or baste layers together to hold flat.

17. Hand- or machine-quilt on marked lines and as desired. When quilting is complete, trim edges even. Bind with self-made or purchased binding to finish. ❖

Two-Part Harmony

BY ALEXANDRA CAPADALIS DUPRÉ

This tessellating design in light and dark flannel pieces looks complicated, but it is actually fairly simple to construct. The quilt is made with only two squares, the larger squares moving down one space in the color order in each row. If you follow the Placement Diagram carefully, your quilt will be in perfect two-part harmony.

Two-Part Harmony

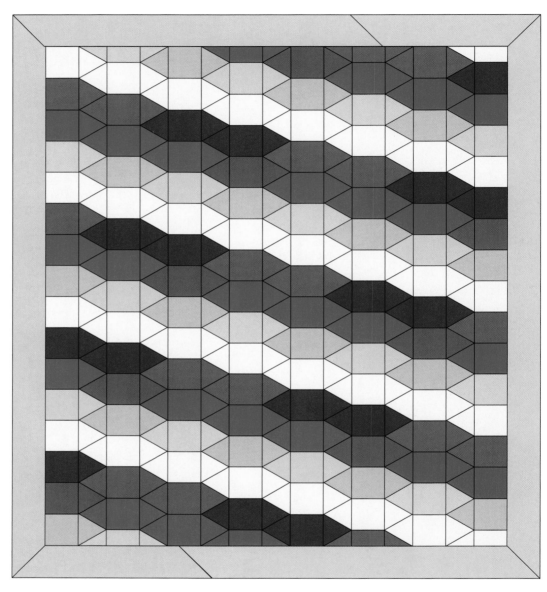

COLOR KEY
- ■ Burgundy prints
- ■ Tan prints
- □ Cream prints
- ■ Green prints
- ■ Rose floral
- ■ Purple print
- ■ Brown prints
- ■ Tan floral

Two-Part Harmony
Placement Diagram
Approximately 48" x 54"

Two-Part Harmony

Project Specifications

Quilt Size: Approximately 48" x 54"

Fabric & Batting

- ⅛ yard each 1 purple and 2 brown flannel prints
- ¼ yard each 2 different burgundy and tan, 3 different green and 4 different cream flannel prints
- ¾ yard each tan and rose flannel florals
- Backing 52" x 58"
- Batting 52" x 58"
- 6¼ yards self-made or purchased binding

Supplies & Tools

- Neutral color all-purpose thread
- Off-white quilting thread
- Basic sewing tools and supplies

Instructions

1. Prepare templates using pattern pieces given; cut as directed on each piece.

2. Join four A squares using one A square from each color family in the order shown in Figure 1; repeat for four different groups referring to the Placement Diagram for positioning of colors. Join the four groups to make a vertical row.

Figure 1
Join 4 A squares using 1 A square from each color family in the order shown.

3. Complete four vertical A rows referring to Figure 2. *Note: The A squares move down one space in color order in each row; color placement is crucial to the design so be extremely careful, referring to the color photo and Placement Diagram often for placement of colored A squares.*

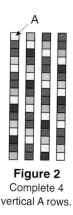

Figure 2
Complete 4 vertical A rows.

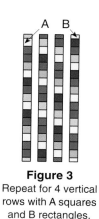

Figure 3
Repeat for 4 vertical rows with A squares and B rectangles.

4. Repeat for four vertical rows with A squares and B rectangles referring to Figure 3 for color order.

Two-Part Harmony

5. Join C triangles in the same color order as the vertical rows referring to Figure 4; sew D and DR to the ends.

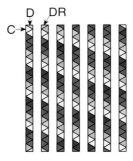

Figure 4
Join C triangles in the same color order as the vertical rows; sew D and DR to ends.

6. Join the A, A-B and C-D rows referring to the Placement Diagram for positioning of rows.

7. Cut and piece one strip each rose and tan florals 3½" x 57"; sew a strip to opposite sides of the pieced center referring to the Placement Diagram for color placement.

8. Cut two strips each rose and tan florals 3½" x 20" and 3½" x 37". Sew a 20" tan floral strip to a 37" rose floral strip with a diagonal seam as

shown in Figure 5; repeat with the remaining strips. Trim excess seam to ¼" as shown in Figure 6; press seam open.

Figure 5
Sew a 20" tan floral strip to a 37" rose floral strip with a diagonal seam as shown.

Figure 6
Trim excess seam to 1/4" as shown.

9. Center and sew the strips to the top and bottom of the pieced center referring to the Placement Diagram for color placement and mitering corners. Trim excess at corners; press seams toward strips.

10. Sandwich batting between completed top and prepared backing piece; pin or baste to hold layers together.

11. Quilt as desired by hand or machine. *Note: The quilt shown was machine-quilted in the ditch of seams using off-white quilting thread.*

12. When quilting is complete, trim edges even and remove pins or basting. Bind edges with self-made or purchased binding to finish. ❖

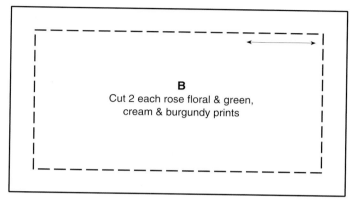

B
Cut 2 each rose floral & green,
cream & burgundy prints

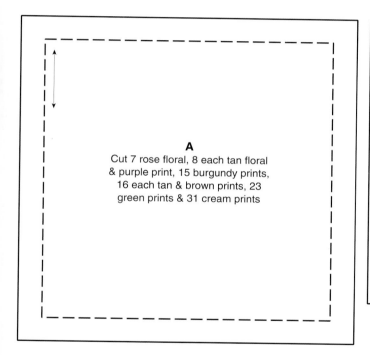

A
Cut 7 rose floral, 8 each tan floral
& purple print, 15 burgundy prints,
16 each tan & brown prints, 23
green prints & 31 cream prints

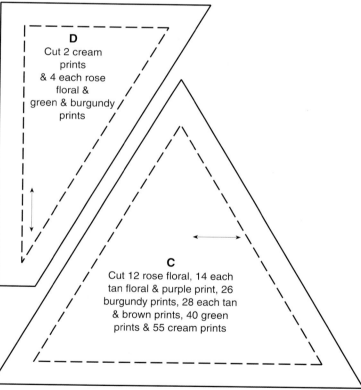

D
Cut 2 cream
prints
& 4 each rose
floral &
green & burgundy
prints

C
Cut 12 rose floral, 14 each
tan floral & purple print, 26
burgundy prints, 28 each tan
& brown prints, 40 green
prints & 55 cream prints

Swirling Triangles

BY RUTH SWASEY

Because each swirling triangle block can be made with a different fabric, this is the perfect quilt for quilters who have scraps collected from past projects. The quilt is made with 88 full blocks and 11 half-blocks, allowing plenty of opportunity for a colorful collection of scraps, or—if you prefer—limit your triangles to two or three different fabrics. Although it might take long to piece, this really is an easy pattern.

Swirling Triangles

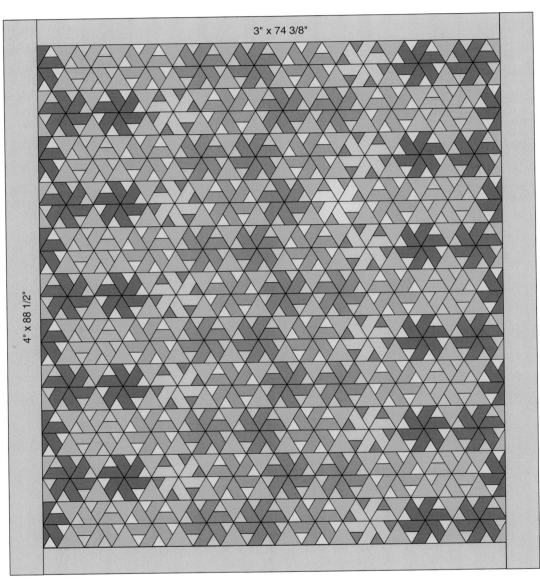

3" x 74 3/8"

4" x 88 1/2"

Swirling Triangles
Placement Diagram
82 3/8" x 88 1/2"

Swirling Triangles

Project Specifications

Quilt Size: 82⅜" x 88½"

Block Size: 7½" x 8¾"

Number of Blocks: 88 whole blocks; 11 half-blocks

Fabric & batting

- 1½ yards total background prints
- 1¾ yards green print for background
- 3 yards total scraps
- 3 yards border print
- Backing 87" x 93"
- Batting 87" x 93"
- 10 yards self-made or purchased binding

Supplies & Tools

- Neutral color all-purpose thread
- Tan pearl cotton
- Basic sewing tools and supplies

Instructions

1. Prepare templates using pattern pieces given. Cut as directed on pieces A, B and C for one block, also cut D as directed. Or, pieces may be cut from strips using templates A/B-C and D given. For A, cut strips 2¼"

Swirling Triangles
7 1/2" x 8 3/4" Block

wide; for B, cut strips 2½" wide; and for C, D and DR, cut 13 strips green print 4¼" wide by fabric width.

2. Sew an A strip to a B strip as shown in Figure 1. Using the C template given marked with lines for A and B, cut pieces from strip, again referring to Figure 1. You will get two different compositions; both may be used.

Figure 1
Sew an A strip to a B strip; cut A-B triangles from pieced strip.

3. Join six A-B units to complete one hexagon block as shown in Figure 2; repeat for 88 blocks.

Figure 2
Join 6 A-B units to
complete 1 block.

Swirling Triangles

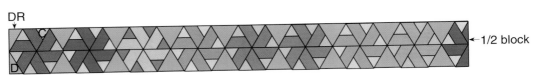

Figure 5
Join blocks to make a row.

4. Make half-blocks using four A-B units and trim ¼" from center seam as shown in Figure 3. Repeat for 11 half-blocks.

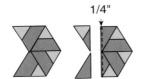

Figure 3
Join 4 A-B units as shown. Trim 1/4" away from center seam for half-blocks.

5. For pieces C, D and DR, using templates given, cut pieces from strips referring to Figure 4. Cut as directed on templates.

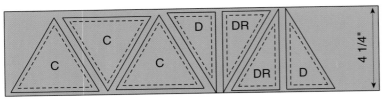

Figure 4
Cut C, D and DR from 4 1/4" strips as shown.

6. Arrange A-B whole and half-blocks with C, D and DR to make a row as shown in Figure 5; join pieces to make a row; repeat for 11 rows.

7. Join rows referring to the Placement Diagram for positioning of rows. Press completed top.

8. Cut two strips border print 3½" x 74⅞". Sew a strip to the top and bottom of the pieced center; press seams toward strips. Cut two strips border print 4½" x 89". Sew a strip to opposite long sides; press seams toward strips.

9. Sandwich batting between completed top and prepared backing piece. Pin or baste layers together to hold flat.

10. Tie quilt layers together at all C points using pearl cotton.

11. When tying is complete, trim edge even. Bind with self-made or purchased binding to finish. ❖

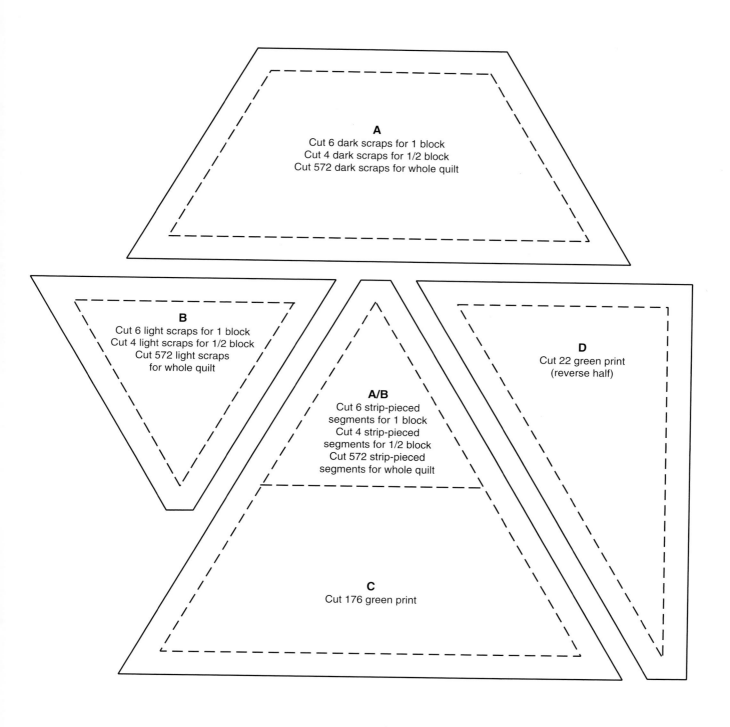

A
Cut 6 dark scraps for 1 block
Cut 4 dark scraps for 1/2 block
Cut 572 dark scraps for whole quilt

B
Cut 6 light scraps for 1 block
Cut 4 light scraps for 1/2 block
Cut 572 light scraps
for whole quilt

A/B
Cut 6 strip-pieced
segments for 1 block
Cut 4 strip-pieced
segments for 1/2 block
Cut 572 strip-pieced
segments for whole quilt

D
Cut 22 green print
(reverse half)

C
Cut 176 green print

A Fondness for Flannel

BY PAT YEO

There are so many gorgeous flannel fabrics available today that you can make this quick and easy quilt in any color of the rainbow. To create a quilt that looks like the one shown, gather all of your brown and beige homespun, plaid and flannel fabrics. Add 10 hearts created from red-and-black check flannel, and you've created a perfectly warm, inviting quilt for anyone to curl up under.

A Fondness for Flannel

Project Specifications

Quilt Size: 57½" x 57½"
Block Size: 5½" x 5½"
Number of Blocks: 81

Fabric & Batting

- Assorted brown and beige homespuns or plaid flannel to total 4½ yards
- ¼ yard red-and-black check flannel
- ⅓ yard tan solid flannel
- ½ yard brown solid flannel
- Backing 64" x 64"
- Batting 64" x 64"
- 7 yards self-made or purchased binding

Supplies & Tools

- Neutral color all-purpose thread
- Freezer paper
- Basic sewing tools and supplies, rotary cutter, ruler and cutting mat

Instructions

1. Cut 81 squares 6" x 6" from an assortment of homespun or flannel plaids.

A Fondness for Flannel

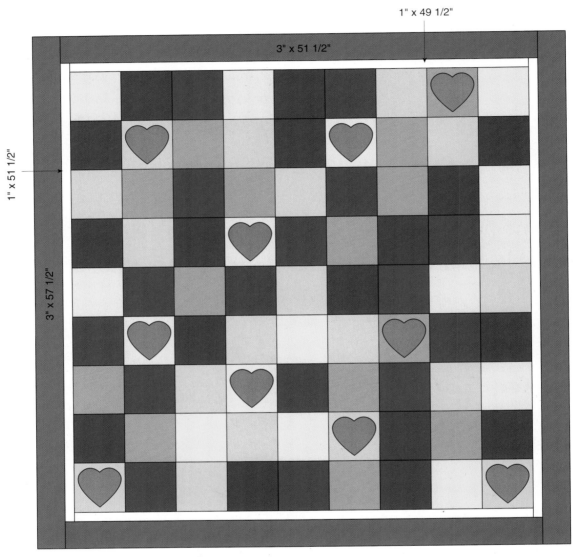

A Fondness for Flannel
Placement Diagram
57 1/2" x 57 1/2"

2. Prepare template for heart shape using pattern given. Trace 10 shapes onto the paper side of freezer paper; cut out.

3. Cut 10 heart shapes from red-and-black check flannel, adding a ¼" seam allowance all around when cutting.

4. Press the waxy side of the freezer-paper hearts on the backside of the red-and-black check flannel hearts.

5. Press under fabric heart edges even with freezer-paper shape; pull freezer paper out after pressing.

6. Center a heart shape on 10 light-colored homespun or flannel squares; appliqué in place by hand or machine.

7. Arrange squares in nine rows of nine blocks randomly placing heart squares as desired.

8. Join blocks in rows; join rows to complete the pieced center. Press seams in one direction.

9. Cut and piece two strips each tan solid 1½" x 50" and 1½" x 52". Sew shorter strips to the top and bottom and longer strips to opposite long sides; press seams toward strips.

10. Cut and piece two strips each brown solid 3½" x 52" and 3½" x 58". Sew shorter strips to the top and bottom and longer strips to opposite long sides; press seams toward strips.

11. Sandwich batting between completed top and prepared backing piece. Pin or baste layers together to hold flat.

12. Quilt as desired by hand or machine. When quilting is complete, remove pins or basting; trim edges even.

13. Bind edges with self-made or purchased binding to finish. ❖

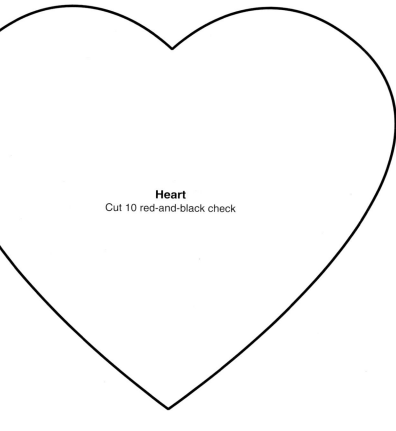

Heart
Cut 10 red-and-black check

Amish Evening

BY MARGARET ROULEAU

Dark fabrics and lots of fine quilting stitches are the hallmarks of the traditional Amish quilt, and this quilt faithfully follows the Amish style. The quilt can be cut and stitched easily using the quick-and-easy methods in the instructions. Although it would seem as if the quilt were made of star blocks, it is actually pieced in units that make a star design once they are put together.

Amish Evening

4" x 80"

8" x 72"

4" x 92"

8" x 76"

COLOR KEY
- Medium teal print
- Black mottled
- Lavender print
- Cranberry print
- Dark teal print
- Blue print
- Navy print
- Boysenberry print

Amish Evening
Placement Diagram
80" x 100"

Amish Evening

Project Specifications

Quilt Size: 80" x 100"

Fabric & Batting

- ⅝ yard each blue, dark teal, lavender, cranberry and navy prints
- 1½ yards each medium teal print
- 3 yards boysenberry print
- 3¾ yards black mottled
- Backing 84" x 104"
- Batting 84" x 104"
- 10½ yards self-made or purchased binding

Supplies & Tools

- All-purpose thread to match fabrics
- Black quilting thread
- Basic sewing tools and supplies and silver marking pencil

Instructions

1. Cut four 4½" by fabric length strips boysenberry print for outside borders; set aside.

2. Cut sixteen 4½" x 4½" squares each blue, dark teal, lavender, cranberry, navy and boysenberry prints for A. Mark a diagonal line on the wrong side of each A square.

3. Cut 17 rectangles medium teal print 8½" x 12½" for B.

4. To piece one A-B unit, place one A square on one corner of B as shown in Figure 1; stitch on the diagonal line. Trim excess to make a ¼" seam allowance as shown in Figure 2; press A open. Repeat with the same-color A on the adjacent corner of B as shown in Figure 3.

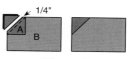

Figure 1
To piece 1 A-B unit, place 1 A square on 1 corner of B as shown; stitch on the diagonal line.

Figure 2
Trim excess to make a 1/4" seam allowance; press A open.

Figure 3
Repeat with the same-color A on the adjacent corner of B as shown.

5. Add two different same-color A squares to the opposite corners as in step 4 referring to Figure 4. Repeat for 17 A-B units referring to the row drawings for color combinations needed. Set aside remaining A squares for A-F units.

Figure 4
Add 2 different same-color A squares to the opposite corners.

6. Cut four 8½" x 80" strips along length of black mottled for inside borders; set aside.

Amish Evening

7. From the remaining black mottled, cut six 12½" x 12½" squares for D, ten 4½" x 12½" rectangles for E, fourteen 4½" x 8½" rectangles for F and four 4½" x 4½" squares for A.

8. Cut two 8½" x 8½" squares each blue, dark teal, lavender, cranberry, navy and boysenberry prints for G.

9. Sew two same-color A squares to two sides of F as in step 4 to make an A-F unit referring to Figure 5; repeat for three each lavender, cranberry and blue units, two each navy and dark teal units and one boysenberry unit.

Figure 5
Sew 2 same-color A squares to 2
sides of F to make an A-F unit.

10. Join two black mottled A squares, two E rectangles and three A-F units to make row 1 as shown in Figure 6; repeat for row 9, again referring to Figure 6 for color placement.

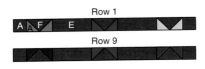

Figure 6
Join 2 black mottled A squares, 2 E
rectangles and 3 A-F units to make
row 1 as shown; repeat for row 9.

11. Join two A-F units with three different-color G squares and two A-B units as shown in Figure 7 to make row 2; repeat for rows 4, 6 and 8, again referring to Figure 7 for color positioning.

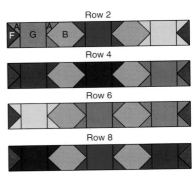

Figure 7
Join 2 A-F units with 3 different-
color G squares and 2 A-B units
as shown to make row 2; repeat
for rows 4, 6 and 8.

12. Join two E rectangles with two D squares and three A-B units as shown in Figure 8 to make row 3; repeat for rows 5 and 7, again referring to Figure 8 for color positioning.

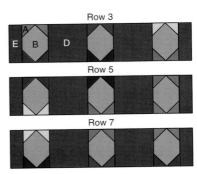

Figure 8
Join 2 E rectangles with 2 D squares
and 3 A-B units as shown to make
row 3; repeat for rows 5 and 7.

13. Arrange the rows in numerical order referring to Figure 9; join rows to complete the pieced center. Press seams in one direction.

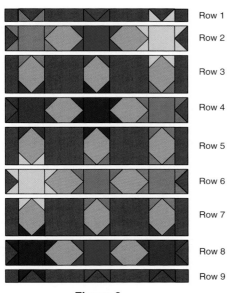

Figure 9
Arrange the rows in numerical order.

14. Cut two strips each 8½" x 72½" and 8½" x 76½" from the black mottled strips cut in step 6. Sew the longer strips to opposite long sides and shorter strips to the top and bottom of the pieced center; press seams toward strips.

15. Cut two strips each 4½" x 80½" and 4½" x 92½" from the boysenberry print strips cut in step 1. Sew the longer strips to opposite long sides and shorter strips to the top and bottom of the pieced center; press seams toward strips.

16. Mark the completed top with a fancy quilting design of your choice using a silver marking pencil.

17. Sandwich the batting between the completed top and prepared backing piece; pin or baste layers together to hold flat.

18. Quilt on marked lines and as desired using black quilting thread. *Note: The quilt shown was machine-quilted in a large feather design on the wide borders, in straight lines 2" apart on outside borders, in a star design simulating the star shapes in the D squares and E rectangles, in a meandering design in the A-B units and other open areas, and in the ditch of seams between units.*

19. When quilting is complete, remove pins or basting; trim edges even. Bind with self-made or purchased binding to finish. ❖

Falling Stars

BY JOHANNA WILSON

This designer chose to make her quilt out of flannel, but you might like to make use of homespun plaids or stripes in a variety of colors. (You might even choose red, white and blue for a traditional patriotic theme.) Because the quilt is made with strips and squares, it can be put together in very little time. The fun part comes in creating the stars and appliquéing them to the squares, giving the appearance of falling stars across the quilt.

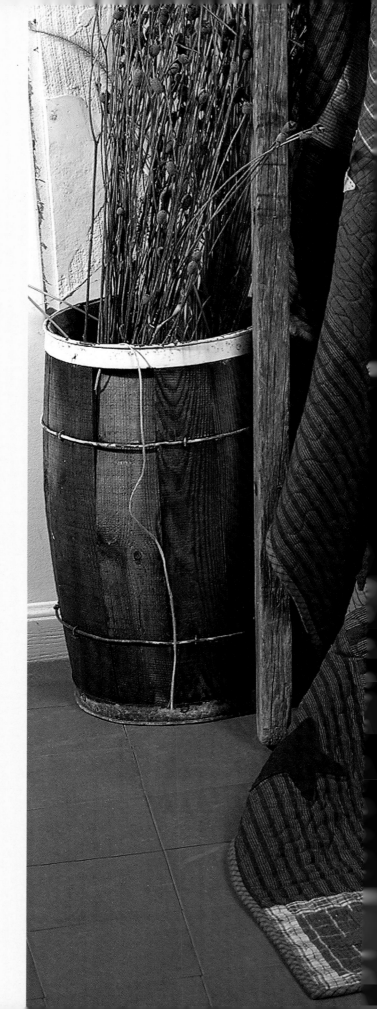

Falling Stars

Falling Stars
Placement Diagram
58" x 70"

Falling Stars

Project Specifications
Quilt Size: 58" x 70"

Fabric & Batting
- 1 yard rust plaid flannel
- 1⅝ yards brown stripe flannel
- Variety of dark plaid and stripe flannel scraps to total 2 yards
- Scraps light, medium and dark wool or felt solids for stars
- Backing 62" x 74"
- Batting 62" x 74"
- 7½ yards self-made or purchased narrow binding

Supplies & Tools
- Neutral color all-purpose thread
- Pearl cotton
- Basic sewing tools and supplies, rotary cutter, mat and ruler

Instructions
1. Cut 43 squares 6½" x 6½" from plaid and stripe flannel scraps.

2. Lay out 15 squares in five rows of three squares each to make the quilt center as shown in Figure 1, positioning colors in a pleasing arrangement. Join squares in rows; join rows. Press seams in one direction.

6 1/2" x 6 1/2"

Figure 1
Lay out 15 squares in
rows of 3 squares each.

3. Cut four strips each rust plaid 6½" x 30½". Sew a strip to opposite long sides; press seams toward strips. Sew the remaining two strips to the top and bottom; press seams toward strips.

4. Join five squares to make a row; press seams in one direction. Repeat to make a second row. Sew to the top and bottom of the pieced center; press seams away from pieced strips.

Falling Stars

5. Join nine squares to make a row; press seams in one direction. Repeat to make a second row. Sew to opposite sides of the pieced center; press seams away from pieced strips.

6. Cut two strips each brown stripe 8½" x 54½" and 8½" x 42½" along length fabric. Sew the shorter strips to the top and bottom of the pieced center; press seams toward strips. Set aside remaining strips.

7. Cut two strips each 1½" x 6½" and 1½" x 8½" light plaid scraps. Cut four 6½" x 6½" squares rust plaid.

8. Sew a 1½" x 6½" strip to opposite sides of a 6½" x 6½" square as shown in Figure 2; press seams toward strips. Sew a 1½" x 8½" strip to the remaining sides of the square, again referring to Figure 2; press seams toward strips. Repeat for four bordered squares.

9. Sew a bordered square to each end of the 8½" x 54½" brown stripe strips. Sew a strip to opposite long sides of the pieced center; press seams toward strips.

10. Prepare template for star shape using pattern given. Cut as directed on pattern.

11. Pin a star shape in each corner square and three on each border strip. Arrange the remaining star shapes on the quilt as desired referring to the Placement Diagram for placement suggestions; pin in place.

12. Using pearl cotton, sew star shapes in place using a running stitch or a buttonhole stitch as shown in Figure 3. *Note: If using wool, it would be helpful to bond some lightweight interfacing to the wrong side of the fabric to avoid future fraying of star shapes.*

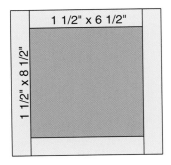

Figure 2
Sew strips to the
square as shown.

Figure 3
Straight-stitch or buttonhole-stitch star shapes in place.

13. Sandwich batting between completed top and prepared backing piece; pin or baste layers together.

14. Quilt as desired by hand or machine. *Note: The sample shown was machine-quilted in a random meandering pattern.*

15. When quilting is complete, trim edges even. Remove pins or basting. Bind edges with self-made or purchased narrow binding to finish. ❖

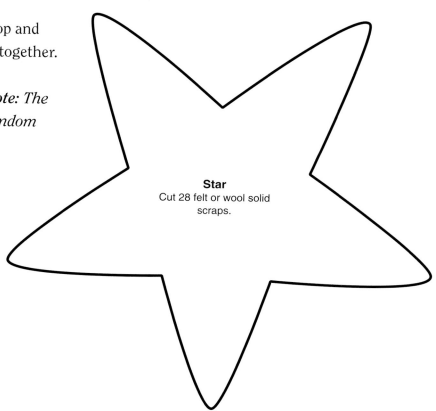

Star
Cut 28 felt or wool solid scraps.

Exotic Petals

BY STITCH 'N CHATTER QUILT CLUB

The Stitch 'N Chatter Quilt Club of Portland, Ind., created this quilt for its annual raffle. The inside petal of each block is made with the same paisley print in four different colors. The other two petals in each color are cut from other fabrics. You can choose to use only three different prints or solids in each color, or a variety of fabrics, as shown in the scrappy version made be Marianna Kreider (see inset photo).

Exotic Petals

4" x 80"

4" x 108"

Exotic Petals
Placement Diagram
88" x 108"

Exotic Petals

Project Specifications

Quilt Size: 88" x 108"

Block Size: 10" x 10"

Number of Blocks: 80

Fabric & Batting

- 1½ yards each blue, yellow, green and pink paisley prints (same print in 4 colors)
- 2 yards total each pink, green, yellow and blue print or solid scraps
- 8 yards cream solid
- Backing 92" x 112"
- Batting 92" x 112"
- 11½ yards self-made or purchased binding

Supplies & Tools

- All-purpose thread to match fabrics
- Off-white quilting thread
- Basic sewing tools and supplies, water-erasable marker or pencil

Instructions

1. Cut two strips each cream solid 4½" x 82" and 4½" x 110" along length of fabric; set aside for border strips.

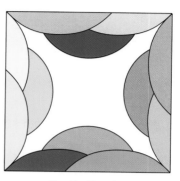

Exotic Petals
10" x 10" Block

2. Cut 80 squares cream solid 10½" x 10½" for background. Fold and crease to mark centers as shown in Figure 1.

Figure 1
Fold and crease to mark center.

3. Prepare templates for pieces A and B using patterns given. Cut as directed on each piece for one block, adding a seam allowance to curved edge when cutting for hand appliqué; mark the centers and overlap lines as indicated on the patterns. Repeat for 80 blocks.

4. Place an A piece of any color on one background square, matching center of piece with center of block

Exotic Petals

as shown in Figure 2. Appliqué in place with matching all-purpose thread, turning under the seam allowance when stitching. *Note: See sidebar on page 61 for curved-appliqué tips. Repeat with three different-color A pieces on remaining sides of the background square.*

Figure 2
Place an A piece of any color on 1 background block, matching center of piece with center of block.

5. Place a same-color B piece on one A piece as shown in Figure 3; appliqué in place as for A. Repeat with a second same-color B piece, matching overlap lines as shown in Figure 4. Repeat on each side of the block, matching B colors with A to complete one block. Repeat for 80 blocks, placing color in same order around background.

Figure 3
Place a same-color B piece on 1 A piece.

Figure 4
Match overlap lines as shown.

6. Mark the centers of each block with the quilting design given using a water-erasable marker or pencil as shown in Figure 5.

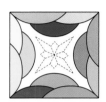

Figure 5
Mark quilting design on block centers, using the 1/4 pattern given.

7. Arrange the blocks in 10 rows of eight blocks each, matching same-color sides of blocks to adjoining blocks as shown in Figure 6.

Figure 6
Match same-color sides of blocks to adjoining blocks as shown.

8. When blocks are positioned as desired, join in rows; press seams in one direction. Join the rows to complete the pieced center.

9. From the border strips cut in step 1, cut two strips 4½" x 80½"; sew a strip to the top and bottom of the pieced center. Press seams toward border strips.

10. From the remaining border strips cut in step 1, cut two strips 4½" x 108½"; sew a strip to each long side. Press seams toward strips.

11. Sandwich batting between the completed top and prepared backing; pin or baste layers together to hold flat.

12. Quilt on marked lines and as desired in border strips, by hand or machine, using off-white quilting thread.

13. When quilting is complete, remove pins or basting; trim edges even.

14. Bind with self-made or purchased binding to finish. ❖

Curved-Appliqué Tips

1. Trace shape lightly onto the right side of fabric.

2. Add a ⅛" seam allowance to each piece when cutting.

3. Clip into curved edge almost to the marked seam allowance as shown in Figure 7.

4. Turn under edge with needle as you stitch, keeping curved edge smooth as shown in Figure 8.

5. Or, make freezer-paper shapes for templates and iron to the wrong side of fabrics. Cut around freezer-paper shapes, adding a ⅛"–¼" seam allowance to curved edges when cutting.

6. Turn edges over freezer paper and press to hold before appliquéing to background.

7. Remove freezer paper through a slit in the background behind each shape either before appliquéing or when appliqué is complete.

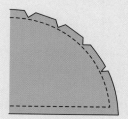

Figure 7
Clip into curved edge almost to the marked seam allowance.

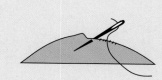

Figure 8
Turn under edge with needle as you stitch, keeping curved edge smooth.

Exotic Petals

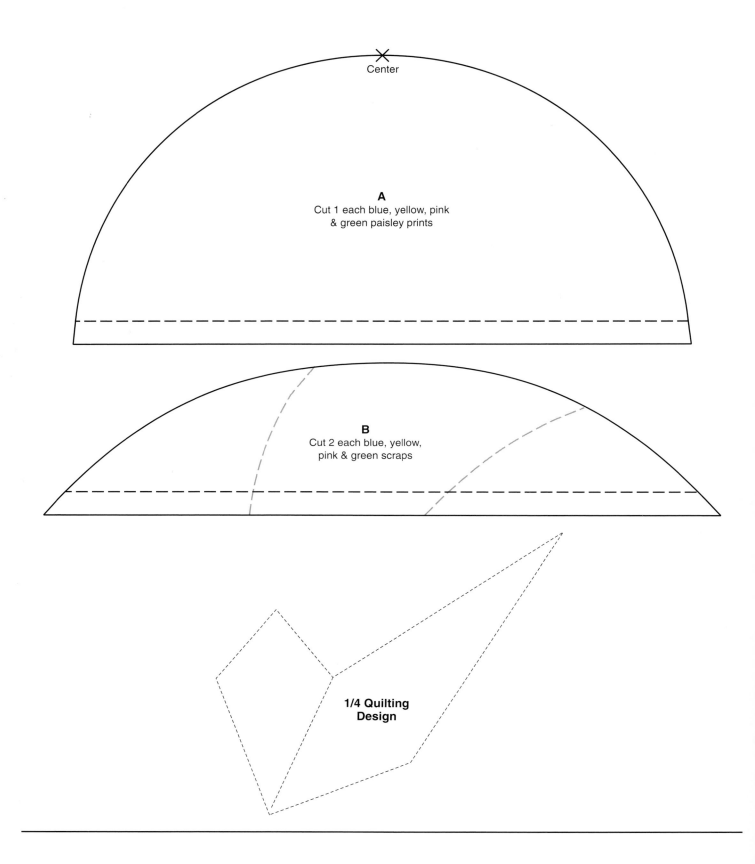

×
Center

A
Cut 1 each blue, yellow, pink
& green paisley prints

B
Cut 2 each blue, yellow,
pink & green scraps

**1/4 Quilting
Design**

Cheery Chore-Time Quilt

BY JILL REBER

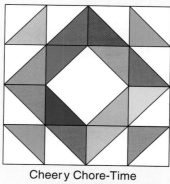

Cheery Chore-Time
12" x 12" Block

Making a quilt is certainly not a chore; especially when you follow these quick cutting and piecing methods. Choose your brightest and cheeriest fabrics to make your quilt, and you'll soon be having the time of your life—instead of a chore.

Cheery Chore-Time Quilt

Project Specifications
Quilt Size: 67½" x 81"
Block Size: 12" x 12"
Number of Blocks: 20

Fabric & Batting
- 1 strip each 3⅞" by fabric width of 15 different nostalgic prints
- 1¼ yards yellow tone-on-tone print
- 1½ yards blue nostalgic print

- 2 yards muslin
- Backing 72" x 85"
- Batting 72" x 85"
- 8¾ yards self-made or purchased binding

Supplies & Tools
- White all-purpose thread
- Basic sewing tools and supplies and ruler

Instructions
1. Cut one strip blue nostalgic print 3⅞" by fabric width. Cut all 3⅞" print strips into 3⅞" square

segments. Cut each square in half on one diagonal to make A triangles. You will need a total of 320 print triangles for A.

2. Cut three strips muslin 4¾" by fabric width. Cut each strip into 4¾" square segments for B. You will need 20 squares for B.

3. Cut 12 strips muslin 3⅞" by fabric width. Cut strips into 3⅞" square segments. Cut each square in half on one diagonal to make A triangles. You will need a total of 240 muslin triangles for A.

4. Sew a muslin A triangle to a print A triangle to make an A-A unit; repeat for 240 A-A units.

5. To complete one block, sew an A triangle to each side of a B square as shown in Figure 1; press seams toward A.

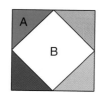

Figure 1
Sew an A triangle
to each side of B.

6. Join two A-A units as shown in Figure 2; repeat. Sew one of these units to opposite sides of the pieced A-B unit as shown in Figure 3.

Figure 2
Join 2 A-A units
as shown.

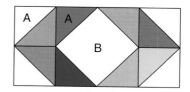

Figure 3
Sew A-A units to sides of A-B.

7. Join four A-A units as shown in Figure 4; repeat. Sew one of these units to opposite long sides of the pieced unit to complete one block; press. Repeat for 20 blocks.

Figure 4
Join A-A units as shown.

Cheery Chore-Time Quilt

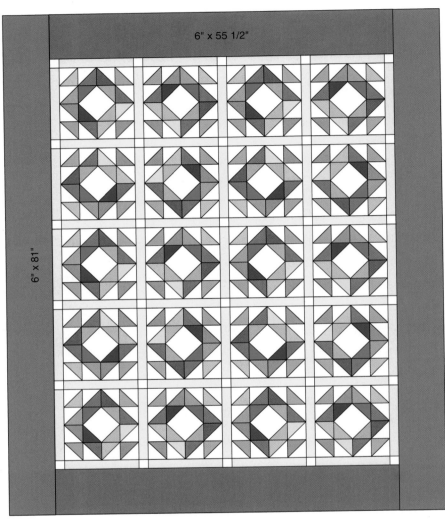

6" x 55 1/2"

6" x 81"

Cheery Chore-Time Quilt
Placement Diagram
67 1/2" x 81"

8. Cut two strips muslin 2" by fabric width; cut strips into 2" segments for sashing squares. You will need 30 sashing squares.

9. Cut three strips yellow tone-on-tone print 12½" by fabric width; cut strips into 2" segments for sashing strips. You will need 49 sashing strips.

10. Join four blocks with five sashing strips to make a block row as shown in Figure 5; press seams toward strips. Repeat for five rows.

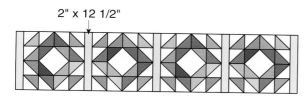

2" x 12 1/2"

Figure 5
Join 5 sashing strips with 4 blocks to make a block row.

11. Join five sashing squares with four sashing strips to make a sashing row as shown in Figure 6; press seams toward sashing squares. Repeat for six sashing rows.

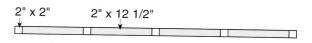

2" x 2"   2" x 12 1/2"

Figure 6
Join 5 sashing squares with 4 sashing strips to make a sashing row.

12. Join sashing rows and block rows beginning and ending with sashing rows; press seams toward sashing rows.

13. Cut and piece two strips each 6½" x 56" and 6½" x 81½" nostalgic blue print. Sew the shorter strips to the top and bottom and longer strips to opposite sides of the pieced center; press seams toward strips.

14. Sandwich batting between the completed top and prepared backing; pin or baste layers together to hold flat.

15. Quilt as desired by hand or machine. When quilting is complete, trim edges even. Bind with self-made or purchased binding to finish. ❖

Seaside

BY LUCY A. FAZELY

This quilt will help you enjoy a trip to the beach long after you have returned home. Simple appliquéd shell shapes—a seashell, a starfish and a sand dollar—in bright colors combine with two quick-pieced blocks to create this seaside memory. Because the appliqué pieces are fused and then machine-appliquéd and the pieced blocks are created with quick-piecing methods, the quilt can be finished in no time.

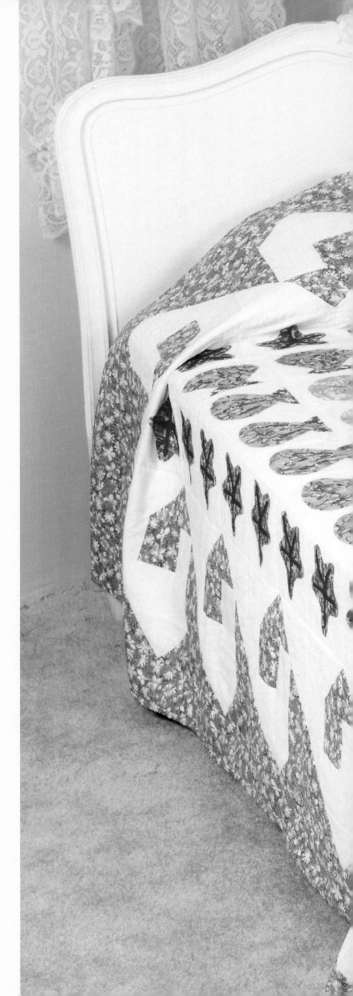

Seaside

Seaside
Placement Diagram
78" x 90"

Seaside

Project Specifications

Quilt Size: 78" x 90"

Block Size: 6" x 6" and 12" x 12"

Number of Blocks: 72 small; 24 large

Fabric & Batting

- ⅜ yard purple print
- ½ yard yellow print
- ½ yard lavender print
- ½ yard red solid
- 1 yard orange print
- 2½ yards blue print
- 4½ yards white-on-white print
- Backing 82" x 94"
- Batting 82" x 94"
- 9¾ yards self-made or purchased binding

Supplies & Tools

- Neutral color all-purpose thread
- Clear nylon monofilament
- 7 yards 12"-wide fusible web
- 4 yards 20"-wide fabric stabilizer
- Basic sewing tools and supplies, template plastic, rotary cutter, mat and ruler

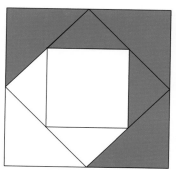

Corner
12" x 12" Block
Make 4

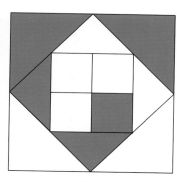

Wave
12" x 12" Block
Make 20

Sand Dollar
6" x 6" Block
Make 16

Seashell
6" x 6" Block
Make 24

Starfish
6" x 6" Block
Make 32

Instructions

Appliqué Blocks

1. Prepare templates for appliqué shapes using patterns given.

2. Trace shapes onto the paper side of the fusible web leaving a margin around each shape and referring to patterns for number needed of each piece. Cut out shapes, leaving a margin around each one.

Seaside

3. Fuse shapes to the wrong side of the fabrics as directed on patterns for color; cut out shapes on traced lines. Remove paper backing.

4. Cut 13 strips white-on-white print 6½" by fabric width; subcut strips into 6½" square segments. You will need 72 squares for appliquéd blocks and four squares for Corner blocks.

5. Center and fuse the seashell, sand dollar and starfish shapes to the white-on-white squares, fusing smaller shapes for each shape onto larger shapes referring to patterns for positioning.

6. Cut 72 squares fabric stabilizer 6" x 6"; pin a square to the wrong side of each fused square.

7. Machine-appliqué shapes using a narrow zigzag stitch with clear nylon monofilament in the top of the machine and all-purpose thread in the bobbin; remove fabric stabilizer when all stitching is complete. Set aside blocks.

Making Wave & Corner Blocks

1. Cut the following fabric-width strips: blue print—three 5⅛" and five 6⅞"; and white-on-white print—three 5⅛" and four 6⅞".

2. Subcut the 5⅛"-wide strips into 5⅛" square segments for A; you will need 24 squares of each color. Cut each square in half on one diagonal to make 48 A triangles of each color.

3. Subcut the 6⅞"-wide strips into 6⅞" square segments for B; you will need 26 blue and 22 white squares. Cut each square in half on one diagonal to make 52 blue and 44 white B triangles.

4. Cut six strips white-on-white print and two strips blue print 3½" by fabric width; sew a white-on-white print strip to a blue print strip with right sides together along length. Press seams toward blue print strip. Repeat for two strip sets. Sew a white-on-white print strip to a white-on-white print strip with right sides together along length; press seams in one direction. Repeat for two strip sets.

5. Subcut each strip set into 3½" segments; you will need 20 white/white segments and 20 white/blue segments. Join two segments to make a Four-Patch center unit as shown in Figure 1; repeat for 20 Four-Patch center units.

Figure 1
Join 2 segments to make
a Four-Patch center unit.

6. Sew two white-on-white print A triangles and two blue print A triangles to adjacent sides of a Four-Patch center unit as shown in Figure 2; repeat for 20 units.

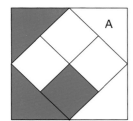

Figure 2
Sew 2 white-on-white print A
triangles and 2 blue print A
triangles to adjacent sides of a
Four-Patch center unit.

7. Sew two white-on-white print B triangles and two blue print B triangles to two adjacent sides of the pieced unit to complete one block referring to the block drawing for placement of colors; repeat to complete 20 Wave blocks.

8. Repeat step 6 with a white-on-white print 6½" x 6½" square used as the block center instead of the Four-Patch unit referring to the block piecing diagram; add three blue print B triangles and one white-on-white print B triangle to complete one Corner block. Repeat for four Corner blocks.

Completing Quilt

1. Join two Wave blocks referring to the Placement Diagram for quilt center.

2. Join four Sand Dollar blocks to make a row referring to the Placement Diagram for positioning of blocks; repeat for four rows. Sew a row to each long side of the pieced center unit and to the top and bottom; press seams toward Sand Dollar blocks.

3. Join six Seashell blocks to make a row referring to the Placement Diagram for positioning of blocks; repeat for four rows. Sew a row to each long side of the pieced center unit and to the top and bottom; press seams toward Seashell blocks.

4. Join eight Starfish blocks to make a row referring to the Placement Diagram for positioning of blocks; repeat for four rows. Sew a row to each long side of the pieced center unit and to the top and bottom; press seams toward Starfish blocks.

5. Join five Wave blocks to make a row referring to the Placement Diagram for positioning of blocks; repeat for two rows. Sew a row to each long side of the pieced center unit; press seams toward Wave blocks.

Seaside

6. Join four Wave blocks for top and bottom rows and sew a Corner block to each end referring to the Placement Diagram for positioning of blocks. Sew a row to the top and bottom of the pieced center; press seams toward blocks.

7. Cut and piece two strips each 3½" x 84½" and 3½" x 78½" blue print. Sew the longer strips to opposite long sides and shorter strips to the top and bottom of the pieced center; press seams toward strips.

8. Sandwich batting between completed top and prepared backing piece; pin or baste layers together to hold flat.

9. Quilt as desired by hand or machine. *Note: The quilt shown was machine-quilted in the ditch of seams using clear nylon monofilament in the top of the machine and all-purpose thread in the bobbin.*

10. When quilting is complete, trim edges even; remove pins or basting.

11. Bind edges with self-made or purchased binding to finish. ❖

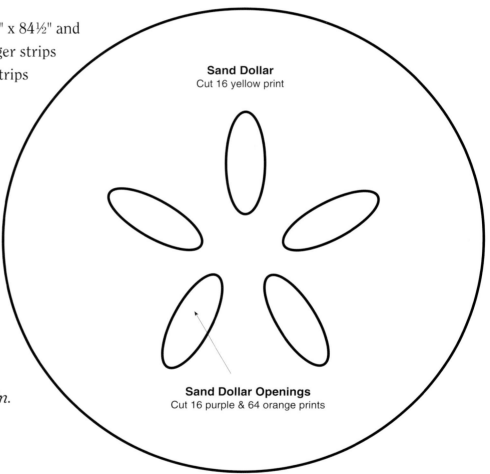

Sand Dollar
Cut 16 yellow print

Sand Dollar Openings
Cut 16 purple & 64 orange prints

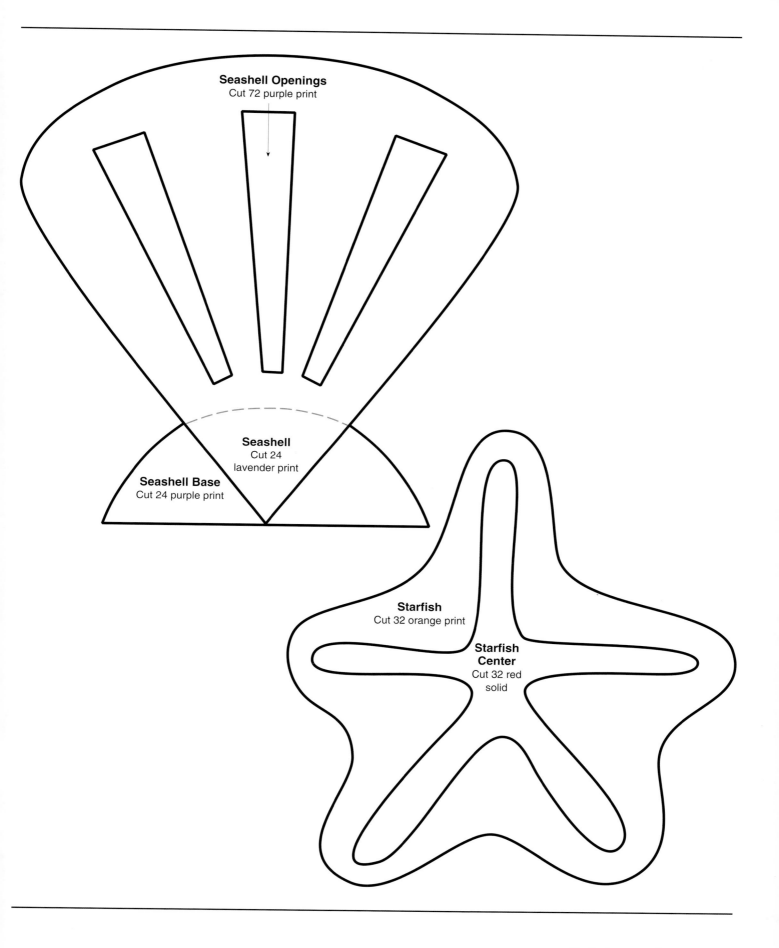

Seashell Openings
Cut 72 purple print

Seashell
Cut 24
lavender print

Seashell Base
Cut 24 purple print

Starfish
Cut 32 orange print

Starfish Center
Cut 32 red solid

Leaf Collage

BY JUDITH SANDSTROM

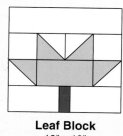

Leaf Block
10" x 10"
Make 13

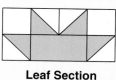

Leaf Section
5" x 10"
Make 20

As summer turns to autumn, leaves turn into a riot of brilliant colors. While Mother Nature combines colors in beautiful blends that are hard to copy, you'll certainly be able to find many fabrics that replicate these autumn colors. Follow these easy cutting and piecing instructions, and you will make a beautiful quilt that celebrates the season but will be appreciated all year long.

Leaf Collage

Project Specifications

Quilt Size: Approximately 72¾" x 92¾"

Block Size: 10" x 10"

Number of Blocks: 33 (13 complete and 20 partial blocks)

Fabric & Batting

- ¼ yard each 16 autumn-colored fabrics
- ½ yard brown print
- 1¾ yards stripe for border
- 2 yards autumn print for border
- 4 yards muslin
- Backing 77" x 97"
- Batting 77" x 97"
- 10 yards self-made or purchased binding

Supplies & Tools

- Neutral color all-purpose thread
- 1 spool off-white quilting thread
- Basic sewing supplies and tools, rotary cutter, mat and ruler

Cutting

1. Prewash and iron all fabrics before cutting. Use rotary cutter, ruler and mat to precision-cut all fabric pieces.

2. Cut the following from muslin: 16 strips 3½" by fabric width; four rectangles 5½" x 10½"; 13 rectangles 3" x 10½"; 26 rectangles 3" x 5"; 66 squares 3" x 3"; and 66 squares 3⅜" x 3⅜". Cut each of the 3⅜" squares in half on one diagonal to make triangles.

Leaf Collage

Leaf Collage
Placement Diagram
Approximately 72 3/4" x 92 3/4"

3. Cut two strips 5½" x 50½" and two strips 5½" x 30½".

4. From the autumn border print, cut two strips 5½" x 50½" and two strips 5½" x 70½".

5. From the brown, cut 12 squares 5½" x 5½", 13 rectangles 1½" x 3", one rectangle 3" x 5½" and two squares 3⅜" x 3⅜". Cut each of the 3⅜" squares in half on one diagonal to form triangles.

6. From each of the 16 autumn-colored fabrics, cut one 3½" by fabric width strip, two rectangles 3" x 5½" and four squares 3⅜" x 3⅜". Cut each 3⅜" square in half on one diagonal to make triangles.

Piecing

1. To make each leaf unit, chain-piece four same-colored autumn-print triangles with four muslin triangles to make four triangle/squares as shown in Figure 1. Trim off points to reduce bulk; press seams toward autumn-colored fabrics.

Figure 1
Stitch triangles to make triangle/squares as shown.

2. Join two triangle/square units with two muslin squares as shown in Figure 2.

Figure 2
Join 2 triangle/squares with 2 muslin squares.

3. Sew a triangle/square unit to each end of the same-colored 3" x 5½" rectangle as shown in Figure 3. Join this unit with the unit pieced in step 2 as shown in Figure 4; repeat to make two leaf units from each autumn-colored print and one brown leaf section for a total of 33 leaf sections.

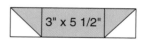

Figure 3
Join 2 triangle/squares with 3" x 5 1/2" rectangle.

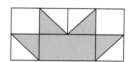

Figure 4
Join the 2 pieced units to make leaf section.

4. To make each stem section, sew a 1½" x 3" brown piece between two 3" x 5" muslin pieces as shown in Figure 5. Press seams toward brown; repeat for 13 stem units.

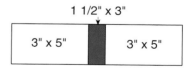

Figure 5
Sew a 1 1/2" brown piece between two 3" x 5" muslin pieces to make stem section.

Leaf Collage

5. Select 13 different leaf sections from the 33 for the center. Make 13 leaf blocks by adding a stem unit to the bottom and a 3" x 10½" muslin strip to the top as shown in Figure 6.

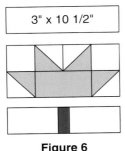

Figure 6
Make leaf block as shown.

6. Arrange the 13 leaf blocks in a pleasing array of colors in three vertical rows—two rows with four blocks and one row with five blocks. Join the blocks in rows.

7. Sew a 5½" x 10½" muslin rectangle to the top and bottom of each four-block row. Join the rows with the five-block row in the center.

8. Sew a 5½" x 30½" strip border stripe to the top and bottom of the pieced center; press seams toward strips. Sew a 5½" x 5½" brown square to each end of the 5½" x 50½" border stripe strips. Sew one of these strips to each long side of the pieced center; press seams toward strips.

9. Stitch six leaf sections together on short ends to make a strip as shown in Figure 7; repeat. Sew a strip to each long side with leaves pointing toward outside edge; press.

Figure 7
Sew 6 leaf sections together to make side strip.

10. Sew four leaf sections together on short ends to make a strip; repeat. Sew a 5½" x 5½" brown square to each end of each strip. Sew a strip to the top and bottom of the pieced center with leaves pointing toward outside edge; press.

11. Sew a 5½" x 70½" strip autumn print to opposite long sides; press seams toward strips. Sew a 5½" x 5½" square brown to each end of the 5½" x 50½" autumn print strips. Sew these strips to the top and bottom; press seams toward strips.

12. Sew a 3½" by fabric width strip muslin to the same-size strip of each autumn-colored fabric along length. Press seams toward darker fabric. Cut each strip in half to form 32 strips 6½" x 22".

13. Join these strips two by two with the leaf fabrics together and muslin strips on the outside as shown

in Figure 8 to make a total of 16 different combinations; press center seams open.

Figure 8
Join 2 strip sections to make a 4-strip unit as shown.

14. Cut each stitched section into 3½" segments as shown in Figure 9. You should get six segments from each stitched section.

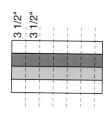

Figure 9
Cut each strip set into 3 1/2" segments.

15. Randomly stitch four different color strips together, matching seams as shown in Figure 10. Cut ¼" away from upper and lower seam points as shown in Figure 11. Stitch five of these sections together for long sides and four for the top and bottom. Add units to ends or remove units as needed to fit strips to quilt edges.

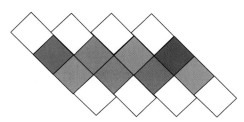

Figure 10
Sew 4 different color strips together, offsetting as shown.

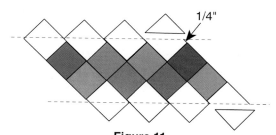

1/4"

Figure 11
Trim excess 1/4" away from upper and lower seam points.

16. Sew a long strip to each side, centering strip so corners end the same on each end; repeat for top and bottom, mitering corners; press seams toward inner border strip. *Note: The pieces at the corners will not be the same width as those across the strip after mitering. You may have to work at the corners to make them fit properly. As with any Seminole-style strip piecing, variations will occur in size of segments when stitching.*

17. Sandwich batting between prepared backing piece and pieced top. Pin or baste layers together to hold flat for quilting.

18. Quilt in the ditch of seams of leaf sections, border strips and squares, and quilt the center in a 3½" diagonal grid or as desired by hand or machine. When quilting is complete, trim edges even; remove pins or basting.

19. Bind edges with self-made or purchased binding to finish. ❖

Southwest Seminole

BY KAREN NEARY

This quilt designer loved her quilt so much that in addition to completing a full-size quilt in the Southwest style, she made a pillow and a miniature version of her quilt as well. The miniature version would look great as a wall hanging in the room with the quilt or in another room that celebrates Native American art. The technique used to make this quilt, called "Seminole piecing," is a quick and fun method of quiltmaking.

Southwest Seminole Quilt & Pillow

Project Specifications
Quilt Size: 68½" x 81½"
Pillow Size: 12" x 12"

Fabric & Batting
- ⅔ yard each cream and turquoise solids
- 1 yard black solid
- 6½ yards sienna solid
- Backing 73" x 86"
- Batting 73" x 86" and 12½" x 12½"
- 9 yards self-made or purchased cream solid binding

Supplies & Tools
- Neutral color all-purpose thread
- Sienna quilting thread
- Polyester fiberfill
- Basic sewing tools and supplies, rotary cutter, mat and ruler

Making Quilt

1. Cut 26 strips sienna solid 2" by fabric width and four strips each turquoise and cream solids 3½" by fabric width. Cut five strips black solid 3½" by fabric width.

2. Sew a turquoise, cream or black solid strip between two 2"-wide sienna solid strips with right sides together along length to make A strip sets as shown in Figure 1. Press seam allowances in one direction.

3. Cut each strip set into 1½"-wide segments to make A segments as shown in Figure 2.

4. Cut 32 strips sienna solid 3" by fabric width and five strips each cream and turquoise solids, and six strips black solid 1½" by fabric width.

Southwest Seminole

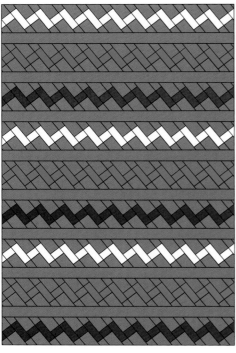

Southwest Seminole Miniature
Placement Diagram
17" x 23 1/8"
(includes binding)

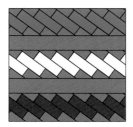

Southwest Seminole Pillow
Placement Diagram
12" x 12"

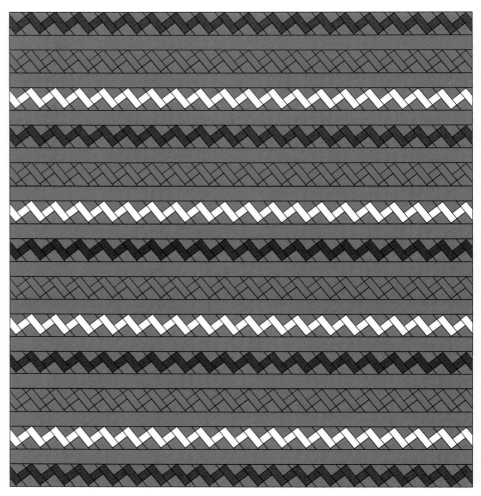

Southwest Seminole Quilt
Placement Diagram
68 1/2" x 81 1/2"

5. Sew a turquoise, cream or black solid strip between two 3"-wide sienna solid strips with right sides together along length to make B strip sets as shown in Figure 1. Press seams in one direction.

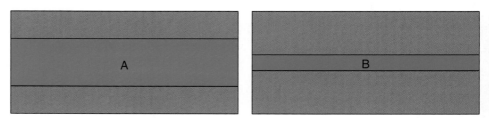

Figure 1
Sew colored strips between sienna solid strips to make A and B strips as shown.

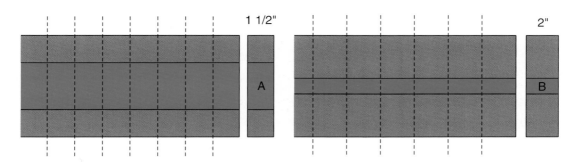

Figure 2
Cut strip sets into 1 1/2"-wide segments for A and 2"-wide segments for B.

6. Cut each strip set into 2" segments to make B segments as shown in Figure 2.

7. Using same-colored A and B segments, sew an A segment to a B segment matching seams of center colored sections as shown in Figure 3; repeat to join 21 A and 22 B segments. Complete four strips each cream and turquoise segments and five strips black segments.

Figure 3
Using same-colored A and B segments, sew an A segment to a B segment matching seams of center colored sections.

8. Trim all strips ¼" past one end point on an A section to square off each end as shown in Figure 4.

9. Trim ½" past top and bottom points; trimmed strip measures 4" x 69". (Leftover A segments may be used to make a pillow following instructions given later.)

10. Cut 12 strips sienna solid 3½" x 69" from fabric length. Sew a strip between pieced strips, arranging color sequence of strips referring to the Placement Diagram. Press seams away from pieced strips.

11. Sandwich batting between completed top and prepared backing piece. Pin or baste layers together to hold flat.

12. Quilt as desired by hand or machine. When quilting is complete, remove pins or basting; trim

Figure 4
Trim all strips 1/4" past one end point on an A section to square off each end.

Southwest Seminole

edges even. *Note: The sample shown was machine-quilted in a zigzag pattern in the solid strips with sienna quilting thread in the top of the machine and all-purpose thread in the bobbin.*

13. Bind edges with self-made or purchased cream solid binding to finish.

Making Pillow

1. Cut two 12½" x 12½" squares sienna solid for lining and backing.

2. Join 11 leftover same-color A segments as shown in Figure 5, offsetting 1". Repeat for one strip each black, cream and turquoise; press seams in one direction.

Figure 5
Join 11 leftover same-color A segments,
offsetting each 1".

3. Trim ends of strips even and ⅜" past points on long sides as shown in Figure 6 to make 3¾" x 12½" strips.

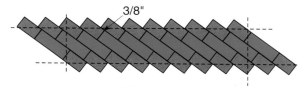

Figure 6
Trim ends of strips even and 3/8" past
points on long sides as shown.

4. Cut two strips sienna solid 1⅝" x 12½". Sew a strip between pieced strips to make pillow top referring to Figure 7; press seams away from pieced strips.

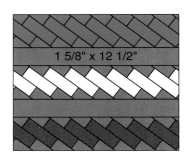

Figure 7
Sew a strip between pieced
strips to make pillow top.

5. Sandwich the 12½" x 12½" piece of batting between pieced top and one 12½" x 12½" sienna solid square; pin or baste layers together.

6. Machine-quilt ¼" from all seams in the pieced strips using sienna quilting thread.

7. When quilting is complete, trim edges even; remove pins or basting.

8. Place backing right sides together with quilted pillow top; stitch around all sides leaving a 4" opening on one side. Turn right side out through the opening; stuff firmly with polyester fiberfill. Hand-stitch opening closed to finish.

Miniature Quilt

Project Specifications

Quilt Size: 17" x 23⅛" (includes binding)

Fabric & Batting

- 1 strip each 5" x 42" black, cream and turquoise solids
- ¾ yard sienna solid
- Backing 21" x 28"
- Batting 21" x 28"
- 2¾ yards self-made or purchased sienna solid binding

Supplies & Tools

- Neutral color all-purpose thread
- Clear nylon monofilament
- Basic sewing tools and supplies, rotary cutter, mat and ruler

Instructions

1. Cut one strip each 2" x 42" black, cream and turquoise solids and six strips sienna solid 1¼" x 42". Sew strips together as in step 2 for quilt. Cut into 1" segments for A segments.

2. Cut one strip each 1" x 42" black, cream and turquoise solids and six strips sienna solid 1¾" x 42". Sew strips together as in step 5 for quilt. Cut into 1¼" segments for B segments.

3. Join 11 A and 10 B same-color segments as shown in Figure 3 for quilt, and trim ¼" past top and bottom points referring to Figure 4 for quilt. Square one end; measure 17" along length of strip and square opposite end as shown in Figure 8. Trimmed strip measures 2⅛" x 17". Repeat for three strips of each color.

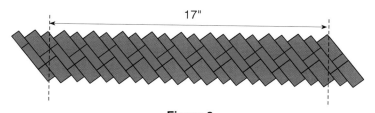

Figure 8
Square 1 end; measure 17" and trim opposite end.

4. Cut eight strips sienna solid 1½" x 17". Sew a strip between pieced strips referring to the Placement Diagram for positioning of strips; press seams away from pieced strips.

5. Finish as in steps 11–13 for quilt, quilting in the ditch of colored strips using clear nylon monofilament in the top of the machine and all-purpose thread in the bobbin for quilt. ❖

Vineyard Stars

BY JUDITH SANDSTROM

Sometimes a beautiful fabric dictates the design of the quilt, and that is the case with this quilt. The designer found a beautiful dark purple and light green tone-on-tone print, which reminded her of grapevines. She cut her star designs from the same fabric, although they look as if they had been cut from different prints. She then added some green and dark purple fabrics to produce this glorious quilt. If greens and purples aren't your favorite colors, don't dismay. This quilt would be a star in any color combination.

Vineyard Stars

2" x 17"

2" x 36"

Vineyard Stars
Placement Diagram
70" x 88"

Vineyard Stars

Project Specifications

Quilt Size: 70" x 88"
Block Size: 11" x 11"
Number of Blocks: 18

Fabric & Batting

- ½ yard each dark purple and light green tone-on-tone prints
- ¾ yard each green-and-purple check and dark purple print
- 2 yards each dark green leaf print and green-and-purple print
- 3½ yards beige-on-beige print
- Backing 74" x 92"
- Low-loft batting 74" x 92"
- 9¼ yards self-made or purchased binding

Supplies & Tools

- 1 spool each natural, dark purple and light green all-purpose thread
- 1 spool off-white hand-quilting thread
- Basic sewing supplies and tools

Instructions

1. Prepare template for piece A. Cut eight A pieces, placing A on the exact same motif on the purple-and-green print fabric. Choose another motif on the fabric; repeat. Continue to make 18 different star

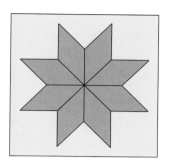

Vineyard Stars
11" x 11" Block

designs, all cut from the purple-and-green print. To make corner star design, cut six A pieces for each unit; repeat for four units. *Note: Each star design appears to be cut from a different fabric, but they were all cut from the purple-and-green print.*

2. Join two exact A pieces along one seam as shown in Figure 1, stopping and starting at marked seam line; repeat for four units. Join two units to make half of the design; repeat. Join the two halves to complete one star design referring to Figure 2; press. Repeat for 18 whole star designs.

Figure 1
Join 2 A pieces as shown.

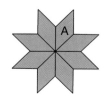

Figure 2
Join A units to complete
star design as shown.

Vineyard Stars

3. Cut 18 squares beige-on-beige print 11½" x 11½". Fold and crease to mark centers.

4. Center one whole star design on each creased square. Turn under the ¼" seam allowance around edges of star design. Hand-appliqué in place to complete one block; repeat for 18 blocks.

5. Cut three strips dark green leaf print 11½" by fabric width. Cut each strip into 2½" segments for sashing strips. You will need 48 sashing strips.

6. Cut three strips green-and-purple check 2½" by fabric width. Cut strips into 2½" segments. You will need 41 of these segments.

7. Arrange blocks with sashing strips and squares in rows referring to Figure 3; join together to make rows. Press seams toward strips.

8. Cut three squares 19⅝" x 19⅝" dark purple print. Cut each square in half on both diagonals to make B side fill-in triangles. Cut two squares 8⅝" x 8⅝" dark purple print. Cut in half on one diagonal to make C corner triangles.

9. Arrange the B and C triangles with the pieced rows referring to Figure 3. Sew to rows; join rows to complete pieced center. Press seams toward strips and triangles. Trim off excess side squares even with outer edges as shown in Figure 4.

Figure 3
Arrange strips, squares and
triangles in diagonal rows.

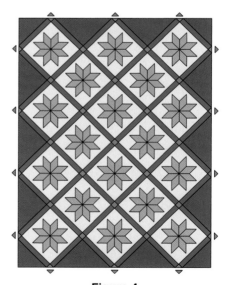

Figure 4
Trim edge squares even with edge
of pieced center as shown.

10. Cut six strips 2½" x 17½" dark green leaf print. Join three strips with two 2½" x 2½" green-and-purple check squares to make a strip. Sew a strip to top and bottom of pieced center; press seams toward strips.

11. Cut two strips 2½" x 36½". Join strips with a 2½" x 2½" green-and-purple check square. Sew another square to each end; repeat. Sew one of these strips to each of the long sides; press seams toward strips.

12. Cut four strips beige-on-beige print 6" x 30". Referring to Figure 5, appliqué three birds and two leaves to each strip, reversing half. Repeat for four strips, two facing left and two facing right.

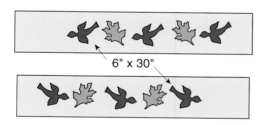

6" x 30"

Figure 5
Appliqué birds and leaves to strips; make 2
left-facing and 2 right-facing strips.

13. Cut four strips beige-on-beige print 6" x 37¼". Appliqué as for strips in step 12 using three birds and three leaves on each strip.

14. Join two A star points; repeat for eight units. Hand-appliqué one unit to one end of each border

strip as shown in Figure 6, placing A diamond units in correct position to match other A diamond units when borders are completed. Sew two shorter strips together on short ends and sew to top and bottom; press seams toward strips.

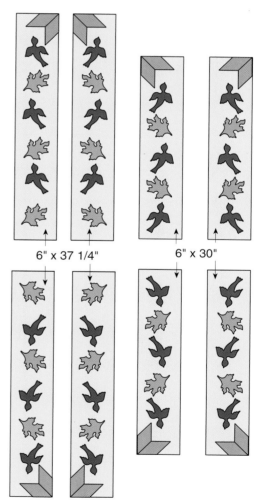

6" x 37 1/4"   6" x 30"

Figure 6
Appliqué an A-A unit to 1 end of each strip.

Vineyard Stars

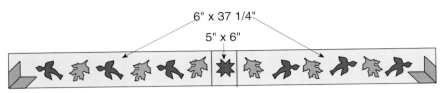

6" x 37 1/4"

5" x 6"

Figure 7
Join 2 strips with 5" x 6" appliqué rectangle.

15. Cut two 5" x 6" beige-on-beige print rectangles. Center and appliqué a small star on each one. Join two remaining border strips with a 5" x 6" rectangle as shown in Figure 7; repeat for second set of strips and rectangle.

16. Cut four squares beige-on-beige print 6" x 6". Join two matching A pieces; repeat for four units. Appliqué an A-A unit to one corner of each square as shown in Figure 8. Sew a matching square to each end of the long border strips. Sew a strip to opposite long sides; press seams toward strips. *Note: The A pieces in each corner should be cut from the exact same location on the green-and-purple print fabric.*

Figure 8
Appliqué an A-A unit to
a 6" x 6" square.

17. Sandwich batting between completed top and prepared backing piece. Pin or baste layers together to hold flat. Quilt as desired by hand or machine using off-white quilting thread. *Note: Quilt shown was quilted in the ditch of strips and around each appliqué shape.*

18. When quilting is complete, trim edges even. Bind with self-made or purchased binding to finish. ❖

Leaf
Cut 20 light green print
(reverse half)

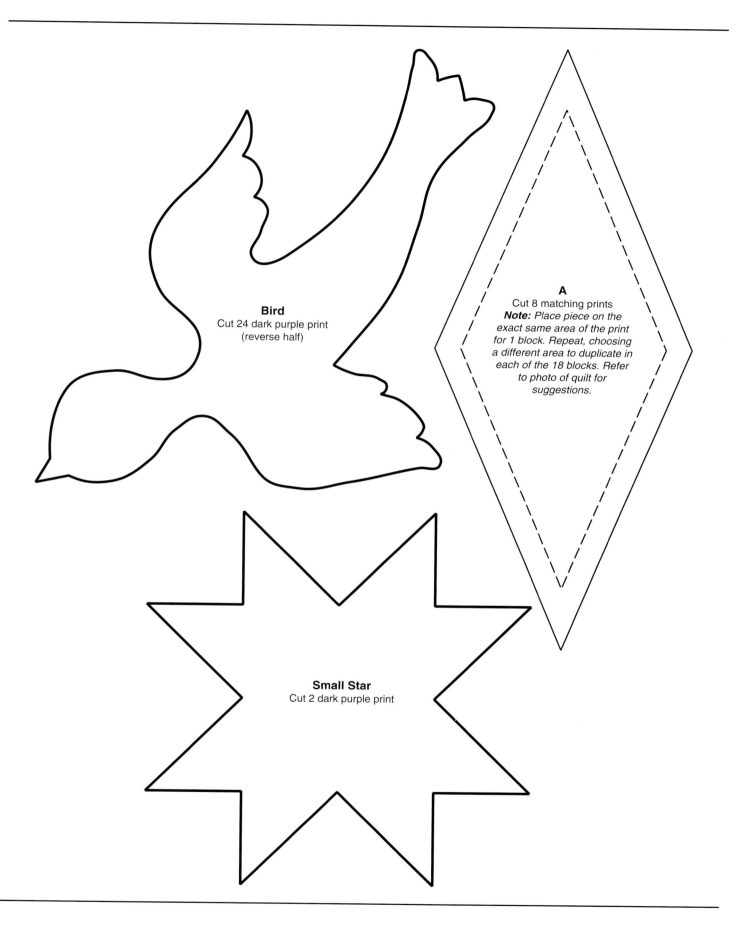

Bird
Cut 24 dark purple print
(reverse half)

A
Cut 8 matching prints
Note: *Place piece on the exact same area of the print for 1 block. Repeat, choosing a different area to duplicate in each of the 18 blocks. Refer to photo of quilt for suggestions.*

Small Star
Cut 2 dark purple print

Anniversary Stars

BY LUCY A. FAZELY

If you like puzzles, you will enjoy putting this quilt together. There are seven different patterns that look very similar but have slight variations. These make up the 36 blocks in the quilt. If you follow the Placement Diagram carefully when joining the blocks, the star designs will appear. Because the outside edges of each block are on the diagonal, be especially careful that you do not stretch the pieces when you handle and sew them.

Anniversary Stars

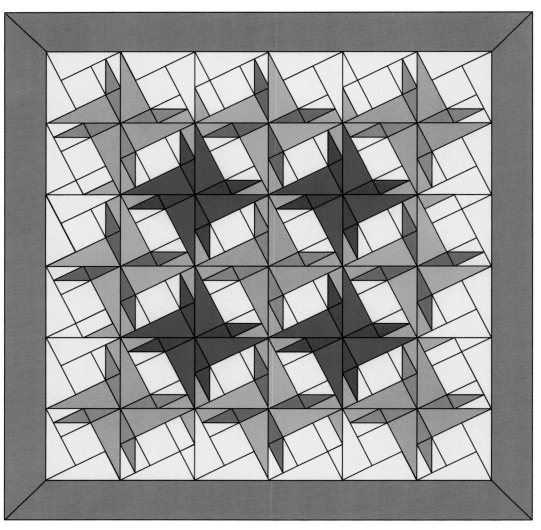

Anniversary Stars
Placement Diagram
72 1/2" x 72 1/2"

Anniversary Stars

Project Specifications
Quilt Size: 72½" x 72½"
Block Size: 10" x 10"
Number of Blocks: 36

Fabric & Batting
- ⅓ yard each multicolored green, blue and red prints
- ⅓ yard each blue and green tone-on-tone prints
- ⅜ yard gold print
- ½ yard tone-on-tone red print
- 2 yards tan print
- 2¼ yards border print
- Backing 77" x 77"
- Batting 77" x 77"
- 8½ yards self-made or purchased binding

Supplies & Tools
- Neutral color all-purpose thread
- Tan quilting thread
- Basic sewing tools and supplies, rotary cutter, mat and ruler

INSTRUCTIONS
1. Cut the following fabric-width strips: three strips tone-on-tone red print, two strips each tone-on-tone blue and green prints and four strips tan print 5 ³⁄₁₆" wide; four strips gold print, three strips each multi-colored blue, red and green print, and six strips tan print 2¹⁵⁄₁₆" wide; five strips tan print 5" wide. *Note: There are no quilting rulers marked in 16ths of an inch. Because we have to be accurate, we try to use the exact size for cutting strips. You might want to cut all strips that are listed in 16ths to the next high-est fraction; for example, 2¹⁵⁄₁₆" would be 3" and 5³⁄₁₆" would be 5¼". Use templates to trim if necessary.*

2. From the strips cut in step 1, cut the following squares and rectangles: 10 tone-on-tone red print 5³⁄₁₆" x 10⅛"; eight each tone-on-tone blue and green prints 5³⁄₁₆" x 10⅛"; 16 tan print 5³⁄₁₆" x 10⅛"; 20 multicolored red print 2¹⁵⁄₁₆" x 5⅝"; 16 each multi-colored blue and green prints 2¹⁵⁄₁₆" x 5⅝"; 24 gold print 2¹⁵⁄₁₆" x 5⅝"; 36 tan print 5" x 5"; and eight tan print 2¾" x 5"; and 36 tan print rectangles 2¹⁵⁄₁₆" x 5⅝" for B pieces.

3. With the 2¹⁵⁄₁₆" x 5⅝" and 5³⁄₁₆" x 10⅛" rectangles all right side up on a flat surface, cut each rectangle in half only in the direction shown in Figure 1.

Figure 1
Cut each rectangle in half.

Anniversary Stars

4. Prepare templates for A and B using pattern pieces given. Place A on each large triangle section and B on each small triangle section and trim off corners as shown in Figure 2.

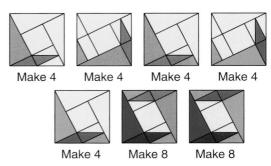

Make 4   Make 4   Make 4   Make 4

Make 4   Make 8   Make 8

Figure 3
Complete blocks in colors and quantity shown in each drawing.

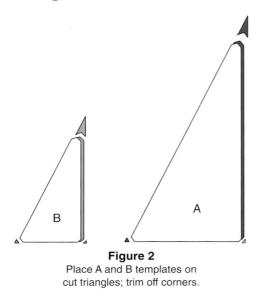

Figure 2
Place A and B templates on cut triangles; trim off corners.

5. Piece blocks as shown in Figure 3, using colors as shown and completing the number of blocks listed. *Note: The outer sides of all A and B pieces are on the diagonal, making all outside edges of each block on the diagonal. Be very careful when sewing and handling blocks not to stretch these diagonal pieces.*

6. Arrange 18 blocks in three rows of six blocks each referring to Figure 4 for block placement. Join blocks in rows; join rows to complete half of quilt top. Press seams in one direction. Repeat for second half of quilt top. Join the two halves to complete the pieced center.

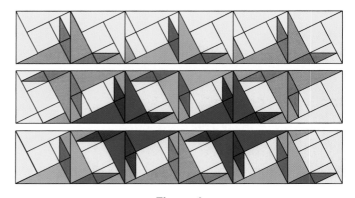

Figure 4
Arrange 18 blocks in 3 rows of 6 blocks each; join blocks and rows to complete half of quilt top.

7. Cut four strips border print 6¾" x 76", cutting each strip from the same identical border motif along the length of the fabric.

8. Fold each strip to find center; crease. Pin to the center of each side of the pieced center, leaving excess at each end. Sew each strip to sides of pieced center. Miter each corner; trim excess on backside of each corner. Press seams open. *Note: If identical strips are cut, each corner motif will be identical and form a unique design where mitered.*

9. Sandwich batting between completed top and prepared backing piece. Pin or baste layers together to hold flat.

10. Quilt as desired by hand or machine using tan quilting thread. When quilting is complete, remove pins or basting; trim edges even.

11. Bind edges with self-made or purchased binding to finish. ❖

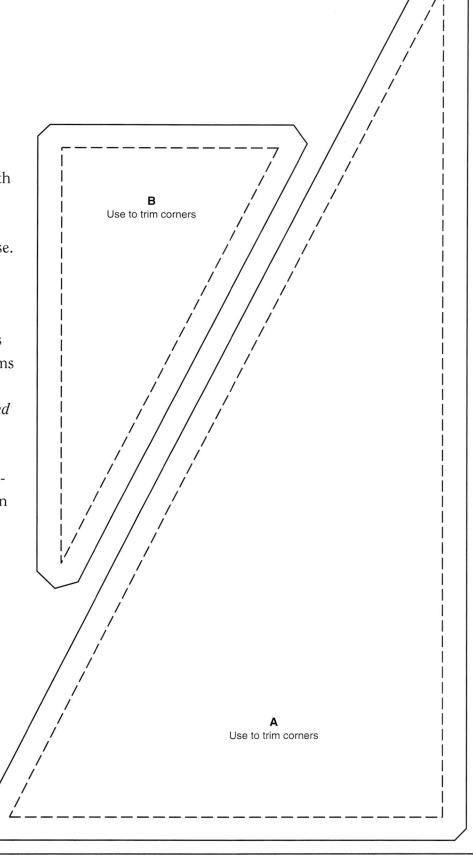

B
Use to trim corners

A
Use to trim corners

Circle of Friendship

BY TONI FIETZ

Combine two blocks and separate them with sashing strips, and you can create this wonderful bed-size quilt that features an interesting pattern. This quilt designer chose to make her quilt in patriotic colors; you can honor your country by using these red, white and blue prints and solids, or you can choose another color combination. Rather than use batting in her quilt, the designer chose to back her quilt with flannel and to attach the flannel to the quilt top with her quilting stitches.

Circle of Friendship

Circle of Friendship
Placement Diagram
88" x 95"

Circle of Friendship

Project Specifications

Quilt Size: 88" x 95"

Block Size: 9" x 9"

Number of Blocks: 36

Fabric & Batting

- 34 strips assorted red prints 1½" by fabric width
- 1¼ yards red solid
- 3 yards 90"-wide white flannel
- 3 yards white-on-white print

- 4 yards navy solid
- 10¾ yards self-made or purchased navy binding

Supplies & Tools

- All-purpose thread to match fabric
- Basic sewing tools and supplies, rotary cutter, mat and ruler

Instructions

1. Cut 35 strips white-on-white print 1½" by fabric width.

2. Sew a white-on-white print strip between two red print strips to make a strip set; repeat for 11 red/white/red strip sets. Press seams toward red print strips. Cut into 1½" segments; you will need 288 segments.

3. Sew a red print strip between two white-on-white print strips to make a strip set; repeat for 12 white/red/white strip sets. Press seams toward red print strip. Cut six strip sets into 1½" segments; you will need 144 segments. Cut the remaining strip sets into 3½" segments for A units as shown in Figure 1.

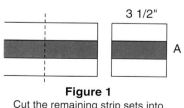

Figure 1
Cut the remaining strip sets into
3 1/2" segments for A units.

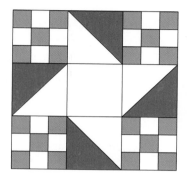

Friendship Star
9" x 9" Block
Make 20

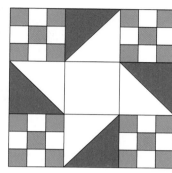

Friendship Star Reversed
9" x 9" Block
Make 10

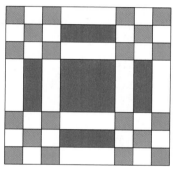

Building Blocks
9" x 9" Block
Make 16

4. Sew a 1½" white-red-white segment between two 1½" red-white-red segments to make a Nine-Patch unit as shown in Figure 2. Press seams in one direction; repeat for 144 units. Set aside.

Figure 2
Sew a white-red-white segment between 2 red-white-red segments to make a Nine-Patch unit.

5. Cut two strips red solid 3½" by fabric width; sub-cut strip into 3½" square segments for B. You will need 16 B squares.

Circle of Friendship

6. Join two Nine-Patch units with an A unit to make a W row as shown in Figure 3; repeat for 32 rows.

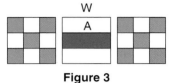

Figure 3
Join 2 Nine-Patch units with an A unit to make a W row.

7. Join two A units with a B square to make an X row as shown in Figure 4; repeat for 16 rows.

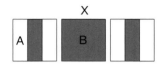

Figure 4
Join 2 A units with a B square to make an X row.

8. Sew an X row between two W rows to complete one Building Blocks block as shown in Figure 5; repeat for 16 blocks.

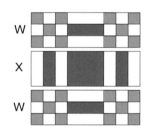

Figure 5
Sew an X row between 2 W rows to complete 1 Building Blocks block.

9. Cut nine strips each red solid and white-on-white print 3⅞" by fabric width; subcut each strip into 3⅞" square segments. Cut each square segment in half on one diagonal to make D triangles. You will need 172 D triangles of each color.

10. Sew a white-on-white print D triangle to a red solid D triangle to make D units as shown in Figure 6; repeat for 172 D units. Set aside 92 units for borders.

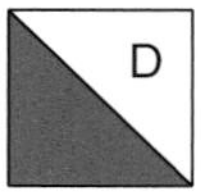

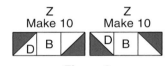

Figure 6
Sew a white-on-white print D triangle to a red solid D triangle to make D units as shown.

11. Cut two strips white-on-white print 3½" by fabric width; subcut strips into 3½" square segments for B squares. You will need 20 B squares.

12. Join two Nine-Patch units with a D unit to make a Y row as shown in Figure 7; repeat for 20 rows each version.

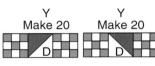

Figure 7
Join 2 Nine-Patch units with a D unit to make a Y row.

13. Join two D units with a B square to make a Z row as shown in Figure 8; repeat for 10 rows each version.

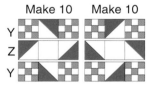

Figure 8
Join 2 D units with a B square to make a Z row.

14. Sew a Z row between two Y rows to complete one Friendship Star block as shown in Figure 9; repeat for 10 blocks and 10 blocks reversed.

Figure 9
Sew a Z row between 2 Y rows to complete 1 Friendship Star block.

15. Cut two strips navy solid 9½" by fabric width; subcut strips into 2½" segments for sashing strips. You will need 30 sashing strips.

16. Join blocks and sashing strips in rows referring to Figure 10. Press seams toward sashing strips.

2 1/2" x 9 1/2" Make 2

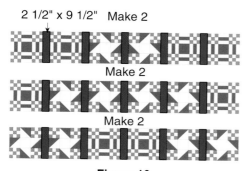

Make 2

Make 2

Figure 10
Join blocks and strips in rows.

17. Cut five strips navy solid 3½" x 64½" along length of fabric. Join the pieced rows with the navy solid strips referring to the Placement Diagram for positioning of rows; press seams toward strips.

18. Cut two strips each along length of navy solid 2½" x 69½" and 3½" x 68½". Sew the narrower strips to opposite long sides and wider strips to the top and bottom of the pieced center; press seams toward strips.

19. Join 22 D units to make a strip as shown in Figure 11; repeat for two strips. Join 24 D units to make a strip as shown in Figure 12; repeat for two strips.

D

Figure 11
Join 22 D units to make a strip.

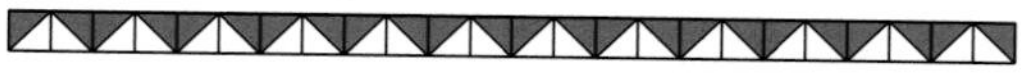

Figure 12
Join 24 D units to make a strip.

20. Cut two strips red solid 2" x 3½"; sew a strip to each end of each 24-unit strip. Sew these strips to opposite long sides of the pieced center; press seams toward navy solid strips.

21. Cut four rectangles red solid 3½" x 4½". Sew a rectangle to each end of each 22-unit strip. Sew one of these strips to the top and bottom of the pieced center; press seams toward navy solid strips.

22. Cut and piece two strips each navy solid 7½" x 81½" and 7½" x 88½". Sew the shorter strips to opposite long sides and longer strips to the top and bottom to complete pieced top; press seams toward navy solid strips.

23. Place the pieced top wrong sides together with the white flannel fabric; pin or baste to hold.

24. Machine-stitch diagonal lines through the centers of each block to hold top and flannel backing piece together to finish.

25. Trim flannel piece even with top. Bind edges with self-made or purchased navy binding to finish. ❖

Stripe Star Quilt

BY JUDITH SANDSTROM

If you prefer the hand- or machine-quilting process to piecing, then this is the quilt for you. The blocks are simple to piece, leaving you plenty of time to put the quilting design on page 109 into the center of each block. The quilt gets its name Stripe Star from the stripe fabric that is used in the sashing and border. If you choose another type of fabric, just call the quilt "Star" because you will be a quilting star when you finish this quilt.

Stripe Star Quilt

2 3/4" x 93"

8 1/2" x 104 1/4"

Stripe Star Quilt
Placement Diagram
93" x 109 3/4"

Stripe Star Quilt

Project Specifications

Quilt Size: 93" x 109¾"

Block Size: 16¾" x 16¾"

Number of Blocks: 24

Fabric & Batting

- ⅜ yard each 9 different red, green, gold and black prints
- 3½ yards stripe for borders and sashing
- 5 yards tan-on-cream print
- Backing 97" x 114"
- Batting 97" x 114"
- 11¾ yards self-made or purchased binding

Supplies & Tools

- Neutral color all-purpose thread
- Off-white quilting thread
- Basic sewing tools and supplies, rotary cutter, mat and ruler

Instructions

1. Cut six strips tan-on-cream print 9" by fabric width; subcut into 9" squares for A. You will need 24 A squares.

Stripe Star
16 3/4" x 16 3/4" Block

2. Cut six strips tan-on-cream print 9¾" by fabric width; subcut into 9¾" squares. Cut each square in half on both diagonals to make B triangles. You will need 96 B triangles.

3. Cut 12 strips tan-on-cream print 4⅝" by fabric width; subcut into 4⅝" squares for C. You will need 96 C squares.

4. Cut four strips of each of the nine colored prints 2" by fabric width.

5. Arrange the 2"-wide strips in 12 random sections of three strips each. Sew three strips with right sides together along length to create a strip set; press seams open. Repeat for 12 strip sets.

Stripe Star Quilt

6. Cut each strip set into 5"-square segments as shown in Figure 1. Cut each square segment on one diagonal to make D triangles as shown in Figure 2. You will need 192 D triangles.

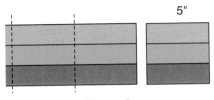

Figure 1
Cut each strip set into 5"-square segments as shown.

Figure 2
Cut each square segment on 1 diagonal to make D triangles.

7. To piece one block, sew a D triangle to each short side of B as shown in Figure 3; repeat for four B-D units.

Figure 3
Sew a D triangle to each short side of B.

8. Sew a B-D unit to opposite sides of A as shown in Figure 4.

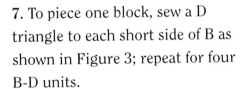

Figure 4
Sew a B-D unit to opposite sides of A.

9. Sew a C square to each end of two B-D units as shown in Figure 5.

Figure 5
Sew a C square to each end of 2 B-D units.

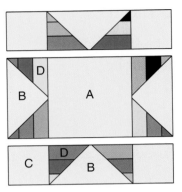

Figure 6
Sew a B-D-C unit to the remaining sides of A to complete 1 block.

10. Sew a B-D-C unit to the remaining sides of A to complete one block as shown in Figure 6; repeat for 24 blocks.

11. Cut 20 strips stripe 1¼" x 17¼". *Note: Cut strips along length, trying to keep the stripe straight along strip.*

12. Join six blocks with five 1¼" x 17¼" strips to make a row as shown in Figure 7; repeat for four rows. Press seams toward strips.

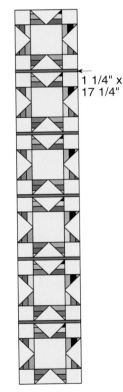

1 1/4" x 17 1/4"

Figure 7
Join 6 blocks with 5 strips to make a row.

13. Cut three strips along length of stripe 3½" x 104¾". Join the block rows with the strips to complete the pieced center; press seams toward strips.

14. Cut two identical strips along length of stripe 9" x 104¾"; sew a strip to opposite long sides of the pieced center. Press seams toward strips.

15. Cut two identical strips along length of stripe 3¼" x 93½"; sew a strip to the top and bottom of the pieced center. Press seams toward strips.

16. Sandwich batting between completed top and prepared backing piece; pin or baste layers together to hold flat.

17. Quilt as desired by hand or machine using off-white quilting thread. *Note: The quilt shown was machine-quilted ¼" away from seams in pieces B and C*

and hand-quilted in the center of piece A using the design given.

18. When quilting is complete, trim edges even and remove pins or basting. Bind edges with self-made or purchased binding to finish. ❖

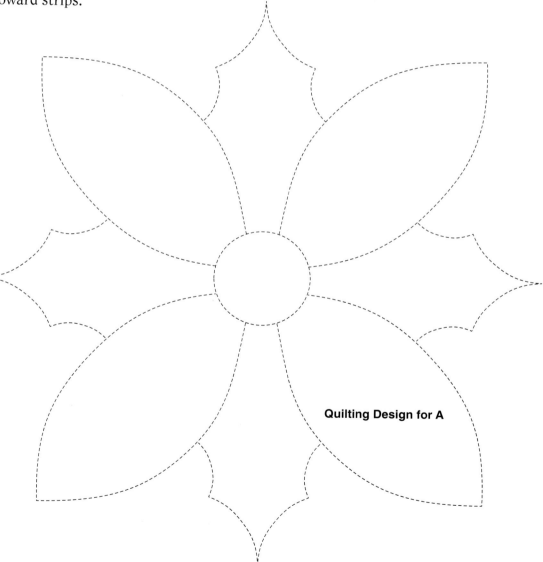

Quilting Design for A

Trailing Blossoms

BY JILL REBER

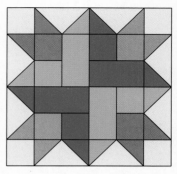

Trailing Blossoms
12" x 12" Block

The blocks in this quilt were the result of a block exchange with the quilter's quilt group. The blocks were put together in this pretty arrangement to create this lovely quilt for her bed. The assorted pinks, purples, dark and light greens are all held together with the choice of a tan print for the sashing and the floral print borders. If pinks, purples and greens are not your favorite colors, try this quilt in other combinations.

Trailing Blossoms

Project Specifications
Quilt Size: 88" x 100"
Block Size: 12" x 12"
Number of Blocks: 34

Fabric & Batting
- 1¼ yards total assorted pinks/roses
- 1¼ yards total assorted purples
- 1½ yards total assorted dark greens
- 1½ yards total assorted light greens
- 2 yards floral print
- 3½ yards tan print

- Backing 92" x 104"
- Batting 92" x 104"
- 11 yards self-made or purchased narrow binding

Supplies & Tools
- Coordinating all-purpose thread
- Water-erasable marker
- Basic sewing tools and supplies, rottary cutter, mat and ruler

Instructions
1. Cut nine strips tan print 2½" by fabric width. Cut into 2½" segments to make A squares; you will need 136 A squares.

Trailing Blossoms

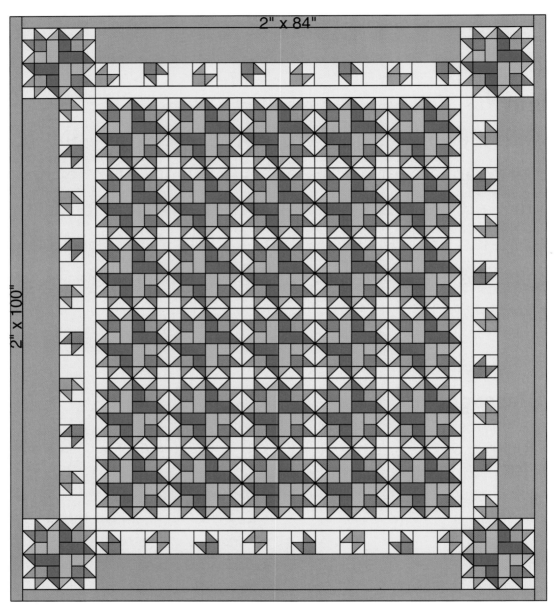

Trailing Blossoms
Placement Diagram
88" x 100"

2. Cut nine strips tan print 5¼" by fabric width; cut strips into 5¼" squares. Cut each square in half on both diagonals to make B triangles. You will need 68 squares to make 272 B triangles.

3. Cut five strips each 2⅞" by fabric width dark green, light green, rose and purple. Cut each strip into 2⅞" squares; cut each square in half on one diagonal to make C triangles. You will need 136 of each color C triangles.

4. Cut eight strips each 2½" by fabric width dark green and light green; cut into 4½" segments to make D rectangles. You will need 68 of each color D rectangles.

5. Cut five strips each 2½" by fabric width dark green, light green, rose and purple.

6. Sew a light green strip to a purple strip along length. Cut into 2½" segments to make A-A units as shown in Figure 1. Repeat with dark green and

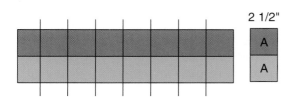

Figure 1
Cut strips into 2 1/2" segments to make A-A units.

rose strips. You will need 68 A-A units of each color combination.

7. Sew a light green/purple A-A unit to a light green D as shown in Figure 2; repeat for 68 units. Sew a dark green/rose A-A unit to a dark green D; repeat for 68 units.

Figure 2
Join units as shown.

8. Sew a light green C and a purple C to B as shown in Figure 3; repeat for 136 units. Sew a dark green C and a rose C to B as shown in Figure 3; repeat for 136 units.

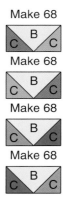

Figure 3
Sew C triangles to B.

9. Arrange pieced units with tan print A squares in rows as shown in Figure 4; join pieces in rows. Join rows to complete one block; press. Repeat for 34 blocks. Set aside four blocks.

Trailing Blossoms

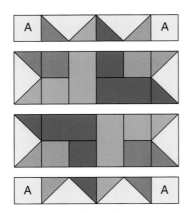

Figure 4
Arrange pieced units with tan
print A squares to make rows.

10. Arrange the remaining blocks in six rows of five blocks each. Join blocks in rows; join rows. Press seams in one direction.

11. To make 16 purple and 18 rose border blossoms, cut three strips tan print, one strip purple and two strips rose 2½" by fabric width; cut into 2½" segments for A. You will need 34 tan print, 16 purple and 18 rose A squares.

12. Cut two strips each rose and purple and three strips tan print 2⅞" by fabric width; cut into 2⅞" segments. Cut each segment in half to make C triangles. You will need 36 rose, 32 purple and 68 tan print C triangles.

13. Sew a tan print C to a rose C; repeat. Sew a rose A to one unit and a tan print A to the other unit as shown in Figure 5; join units to complete one border blossom as shown in Figure 5. Repeat for 18 rose units and 16 purple units.

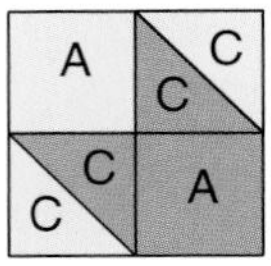

Figure 5
Join units to complete
1 border blossom unit.

14. Cut four strips tan print 4½" by fabric width; cut into 4½" segments for E squares. You will need 32 E squares.

15. Join nine E squares with five rose and four purple border blossom units to make a side border strip as shown in Figure 6; repeat for two strips.

Top and bottom strips; make 2.

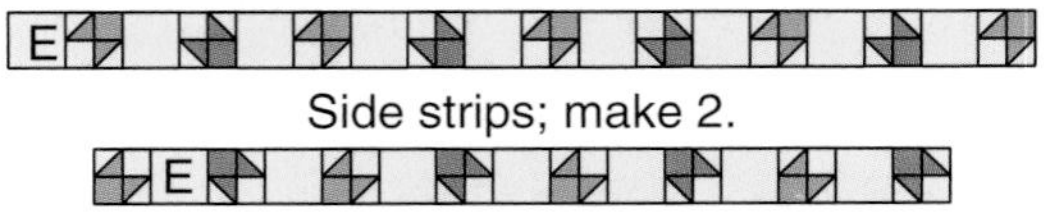

Side strips; make 2.

Figure 6
Join E squares with border blossom units
to make border strips as shown.

16. Join seven E squares with four each rose and purple border blossom units to make a top and bottom border strip as shown in Figure 6; repeat for two strips.

17. Cut and piece two strips each tan print 2½" x 60½" and floral print 6½" x 60½". Sew a tan print strip to a top border strip to a floral print strip to make a top border unit referring to Figure 7; repeat for bottom border unit. Sew strips to top and bottom of pieced center referring to Placement Diagram; press seams toward strips.

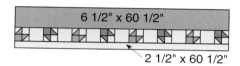

Figure 7
Join strips as shown to make top and bottom border strips.

18. Cut and piece two strips each tan print 2½" x 72½" and floral print 6½" x 72½". Sew a tan print strip to a side border strip to a floral print strip to make a side border unit referring to Figure 8; repeat. Sew a pieced block to each end of each strip. Sew to opposite long sides of pieced center. Press seams toward strips.

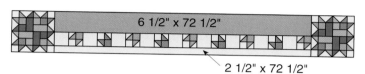

Figure 8
Join blocks with strips as shown to make side border strips.

19. Cut and piece two strips each floral print 2½" x 84½" and 2½" x 100½". Sew shorter strips to the top and bottom of the pieced center and the longer strips to each side; press seams toward strips.

20. Mark top with chosen quilting design using water-erasable marker.

21. Sandwich batting between completed top and prepared backing piece. Pin or baste layers together to hold flat for quilting.

22. Quilt as desired by hand or machine. When quilting is complete, trim edges even. Bind with self-made or purchased binding to finish. ❖

General Instructions

Quiltmaking Basics

Materials & Supplies

Fabrics

Fabric Choices. Quilts and quilted projects combine fabrics of many types. Use same-fiber-content fabrics when making quilted items, if possible.

Buying Fabrics. One hundred percent cotton fabrics are recommended for making quilts. Choose colors similar to those used in the quilts shown or colors of your own preference. Most quilt designs depend more on contrast of values than on the colors used to create the design.

Preparing the Fabric for Use. Fabrics may be prewashed depending on your preference. Whether you prewash or not, be sure your fabrics are colorfast and won't run onto each other when washed after use.

Fabric Grain. Fabrics are woven with threads going in a crosswise and lengthwise direction. The threads cross at right angles—the more threads per inch, the stronger the fabric.

The crosswise threads will stretch a little. The lengthwise threads will not stretch at all. Cutting the fabric at a 45-degree angle to the crosswise and lengthwise threads produces a bias edge which stretches a great deal when pulled (Figure 1).

If templates are given with patterns in this book, pay careful attention to the grain lines marked with arrows. These arrows indicate that the piece should be placed on the lengthwise grain with the arrow running on one thread. Although it is not necessary to examine the fabric and find a thread to match to, it is important to try to place the arrow with the lengthwise grain of the fabric (Figure 2).

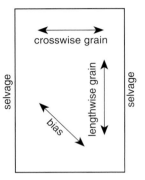

Figure 1
Drawing shows lengthwise, crosswise and bias threads.

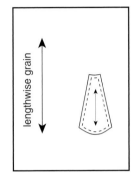

Figure 2
Place the template with marked arrow on the lengthwise grain of the fabric.

Thread

For most piecing, good-quality cotton or cotton-covered polyester is the thread of choice. Inexpensive polyester threads are not recommended because they can cut the fibers of cotton fabrics.

Choose a color thread that will match or blend with the fabrics in your quilt. For projects pieced with dark and light color fabrics choose a neutral thread color, such as a medium gray, as a compromise between colors. Test by pulling a sample seam.

Batting

Batting is the material used to give a quilt loft or thickness. It also adds warmth.

Batting size is listed in inches for each pattern to reflect the size needed to complete the quilt according to the instructions. Purchase the size large enough to cut the size you need for the quilt of your choice.

Some qualities to look for in batting are drapability, resistance to fiber migration, loft and softness.

Tools & Equipment

There are few truly essential tools and little equipment required for quiltmaking. Basics include needles (hand-sewing and quilting betweens), pins (long, thin, sharp pins are best), sharp scissors or shears, a thimble, template materials (plastic or cardboard), marking tools (chalk marker, water-erasable pen and a No. 2 pencil are a few) and a quilting frame or hoop. For piecing and/or quilting by machine, add a sewing machine to the list.

Other sewing basics such as a seam ripper, pincushion, measuring tape and an iron are also necessary. For choosing colors or quilting designs for your quilt, or for designing your own quilt, it is helpful to have on hand graph paper, tracing paper, colored pencils or markers and a ruler.

For making strip-pieced quilts, a rotary cutter, mat and specialty rulers are often used. We recommend an ergonomic rotary cutter, a large self-healing mat and several rulers. If you can choose only one size, a 6" x 24" marked in ⅛" or ¼" increments is recommended.

Construction Methods

Traditional Templates. While some quilt instructions in this book use rotary-cut strips and quick sewing methods, many patterns require a template. Templates are like the pattern pieces used to sew a garment. They are used to cut the fabric pieces that make up the quilt top. There are two types—templates that include a ¼" seam allowance and those that don't.

Choose the template material and the pattern. Transfer the pattern shapes to the template material with a sharp No. 2 lead pencil. Write the pattern name, piece letter or number, grain line and number to cut for one block or whole quilt on each piece as shown in Figure 3.

Some patterns require a reversed piece (Figure 4). These patterns are labeled with an R after the piece letter; for example, B and BR. To reverse a template, first cut it with the labeled side up and then with the labeled side down. Compare these to the right and left fronts of a blouse. When making a garment, you accomplish reversed pieces when cutting the pattern on two

layers of fabric placed with right sides together. This can be done when cutting templates as well.

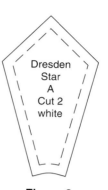

Figure 3
Mark each template with the pattern name and piece identification.

Figure 4
This pattern uses reversed pieces.

If cutting one layer of fabric at a time, first trace the template onto the backside of the fabric with the marked side down; turn the template over with the marked side up to make reverse pieces.

Hand-Piecing Basics. When hand-piecing it is easier to begin with templates that do not include the ¼" seam allowance. Place the template on the wrong side of the fabric, lining up the marked grain line with lengthwise or crosswise fabric grain. If the piece does not have to be reversed, place with labeled side up. Trace around shape; move, leaving ½" between the shapes, and mark again.

When you have marked the appropriate number of pieces, cut out pieces, leaving ¼" beyond marked line all around each piece.

To join two units, place the patches with right sides together. Stick a pin in at the beginning of the seam through both fabric patches, matching the beginning points (Figure 5); for hand-piecing, the seam begins on the traced line, not at the edge of the fabric (see Figure 6).

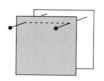

Figure 5
Stick a pin through fabrics to match the beginning of the seam.

Figure 6
Begin hand-piecing at seam, not at the edge of the fabric. Continue stitching along seam line.

General Instructions

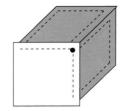

Figure 9
Continue stitching the adjacent side of the square to the next diamond shape in 1 seam from center to outside as shown.

Thread a sharp needle; knot one strand of the thread at the end. Remove the pin and insert the needle in the hole; make a short stitch and then a backstitch right over the first stitch. Continue making short stitches with several stitches on the needle at one

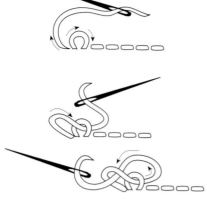

Figure 7
Make a loop in backstitch to make a knot.

time. As you stitch, check the back piece often to assure accurate stitching on the seam line. Take a stitch at the end of the seam; backstitch and knot at the same time as shown in Figure 7. Seams on hand-pieced fabric patches may be finger-pressed toward the darker fabric.

To sew units together, pin fabric patches together, matching seams. Sew as above except where seams meet; at these intersections, backstitch, go through seam to next piece and backstitch again to secure seam joint.

Not all pieced blocks can be stitched with straight seams or in rows. Some patterns require set-in pieces. To begin a set-in seam, pin one side of the square to the proper side of the star point with right sides together, matching corners. Start stitching at the seam line on the outside point; stitch on the marked seam line to the end of the seam line at the center referring to Figure 8.

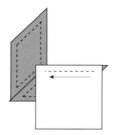

Figure 8
To set a square into a diamond point, match seams and stitch from outside edge to center.

Bring around the adjacent side and pin to the next star point, matching seams. Continue the stitching line from the adjacent seam through corners and to the outside edge of the square as shown in Figure 9.

Machine-Piecing. If making templates, include the ¼" seam allowance on the template for machine-piecing. Place template on the wrong side of the fabric as for hand-piecing except butt pieces against one another when tracing.

Set machine on 2.5 or 12–15 stitches per inch. Join pieces as for hand-piecing for set-in seams; but for other straight seams, begin and end sewing at the end of the fabric patch sewn as shown in Figure 10. No backstitching is necessary when machine-stitching.

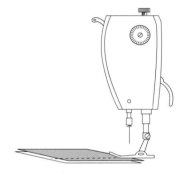

Figure 10
Begin machine-piecing at the end of the piece, not at the end of the seam.

Join units as for hand-piecing referring to the piecing diagrams where needed. Chain piecing (Figure 11—sewing several like units before sewing other units) saves time by eliminating beginning and ending stitches.

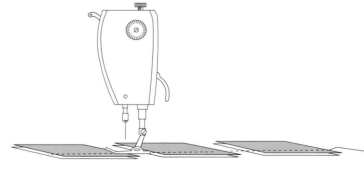

Figure 11
Units may be chain-pieced to save time.

When joining machine-pieced units, match seams against each other with seam allowances pressed in opposite directions to reduce bulk and make perfect matching of seams possible (Figure 12).

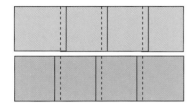

Figure 12
Sew machine-pieced units with seams
pressed in opposite directions.

Quick-Cutting. Templates can be completely eliminated when using a rotary cutter with a plastic ruler and mat to cut fabric strips.

When rotary-cutting strips, straighten raw edges of fabric by folding fabric in fourths across the width as shown in Figure 13. Press down flat; place ruler on fabric square with edge of fabric and make one cut from the folded edge to the outside edge. If strips are not straightened, a wavy strip will result as shown in Figure 14.

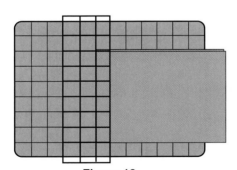

Figure 13
Fold fabric and straighten as shown.

Figure 14
Wavy strips result if fabric is not straightened before cutting.

Always cut away from your body, holding the ruler firmly with the non-cutting hand. Keep fingers away from the edge of the ruler as it is easy for the rotary cutter to slip and jump over the edge of the ruler if cutting is not properly done.

If a square is required for the pattern, it can be subcut from a strip as shown in Figure 15.

Figure 15
If cutting squares, cut proper-width strip into same-width segments.
Here, a 2" strip is cut into 2" segments to create 2" squares. These
squares finish at 1 1/2" when sewn.

If you need right triangles with the straight grain on the short sides, you can use the same method, but you need to figure out how wide to cut the strip. Measure the finished size of one short side of the triangle. Add ⅞" to this size for seam allowance. Cut fabric strips this width; cut the strips into the same increment to create squares. Cut the squares on the diagonal to produce triangles. For example, if you need a triangle with a 2" finished height, cut the strips 2⅞" by the width of the fabric. Cut the strips into 2⅞" squares. Cut each square on the diagonal to produce the correct-size triangle with the grain on the short sides (Figure 16).

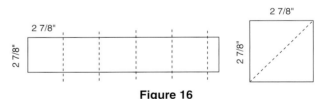

Figure 16
Cut 2" (finished size) triangles from 2 7/8" squares as shown.

Triangles sewn together to make squares are called half-square triangles or triangle/squares. When joined, the triangle/square unit has the straight of grain on all outside edges of the block.

Another method of making triangle/squares is shown in Figure 17. Layer two squares with right sides together; draw a diagonal line through the center. Stitch ¼" on both sides of the line.

General Instructions

Cut apart on the drawn line to reveal two stitched triangle/squares.

Figure 17
Mark a diagonal line on the square; stitch 1/4" on each side of the line. Cut on line to reveal stitched triangle/squares.

If you need triangles with the straight of grain on the diagonal, such as for fill-in triangles on the outside edges of a diagonal-set quilt, the procedure is a bit different.

To make these triangles, a square is cut on both diagonals; thus, the straight of grain is on the longest or diagonal side (Figure 18). To figure out the size to cut the square, add 1¼" to the needed finished size of the longest side of the triangle. For example, if you need a triangle with a 12" finished diagonal, cut a 13¼" square.

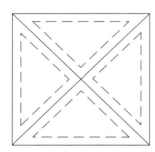

Figure 18
Add 1 1/4" to the finished size of the longest side of the triangle needed and cut on both diagonals to make a quarter-square triangle.

If templates are given, use their measurments to cut fabric strips to correspond with that measurement. The template may be used on the strip to cut pieces quickly. Strip cutting works best for squares, triangles, rectangles and diamonds. Odd-shaped templates are difficult to cut in multiple layers or using a rotary cutter.

Quick-Piecing Method.
Lay pieces to be joined under the presser foot of the sewing machine right sides together. Sew an exact ¼" seam allowance to the end of the piece; place another unit right next to the first one and continue sewing, adding a piece after every stitched piece, until all of the pieces are used up (Figure 19).

Figure 19
Sew pieces together in a chain.

When sewing is finished, cut threads joining the pieces apart. Press seam toward the darker fabric.

Appliqué

Appliqué. Appliqué is the process of applying one piece of fabric on top of another for decorative or functional purposes.

Making Templates. Most appliqué designs given here are shown as full-size drawings for the completed designs. The drawings show dotted lines to indicate where one piece overlaps another. Other marks indicate placement of embroidery stitches for decorative purposes such as eyes, lips, flowers, etc.

For hand appliqué, trace each template onto the right side of the fabric with template right side up. Cut around shape, adding a ⅛"–¼" seam allowance.

Before the actual appliqué process begins, cut the background block. If you have a full-size drawing of the design, it might help you to draw on the background block to help with placement.

Transfer the design to a large piece of tracing paper. Place the paper on top of the design; use masking tape to hold in place. Trace design onto paper.

If you don't have a light box, tape the pattern on a window; center the background block on top and tape in place. Trace the design onto the background block with a water-erasable marker or light lead or chalk pencil. This drawing will mark exactly where the fabric pieces should be placed on the background block.

Hand Appliqué. Traditional hand appliqué uses a template made from the desired finished shape without seam allowance added.

After fabric is prepared, trace the desired shape onto the right side of the fabric with a water-erasable marker or light lead or chalk pencil. Leave at least ½" between design motifs when tracing to allow for the seam allowance when cutting out the shapes.

When the desired number of shapes needed has been drawn on the fabric pieces, cut out shapes leaving ⅛"–¼" all around drawn line for turning under.

Turn the shape's edges over on the drawn or stitched line. When turning in concave curves, clip to seams and baste the seam allowance over as shown in Figure 20.

Figure 20
Concave curves should be clipped before turning as shown.

During the actual appliqué process, you may be layering one shape on top of another. Where two fabrics overlap, the underneath piece does not have to be turned under or stitched down.

If possible, trim away the underneath fabric when the block is finished by carefully cutting away the background from underneath and then cutting away unnecessary layers to reduce bulk and avoid shadows from darker fabrics showing through on light fabrics.

For hand appliqué, position the fabric shapes on the background block and pin or baste them in place. Using a blind stitch or appliqué stitch, sew pieces in place with matching thread and small stitches. Start with background pieces first and work up to foreground pieces. Appliqué the pieces in place on the background in numerical order, if given, layering as necessary.

Machine Appliqué. There are several products available to help make the machine-appliqué process easier and faster.

Fusible transfer web is a commercial product similar to iron-on interfacings except it has two sticky sides. It is used to adhere appliqué shapes to the background with heat. Paper is adhered to one side of the web.

To use, reverse pattern and draw shapes onto the paper side of the web; cut, leaving a margin around each shape. Place on the wrong side of the chosen fabric; fuse in place referring to the manufacturer's instructions. Cut out shapes on the drawn line. Peel off the paper and fuse in place on the background fabric. Transfer any detail lines to the fabric shapes. This process adds a little bulk or stiffness to the appliquéd shape and makes hand-quilting through the layers difficult.

For successful machine appliqué a tear-off stabilizer is recommended. This product is placed under the background fabric while machine appliqué is being done. It is torn away when the work is finished. This kind of stabilizer keeps the background fabric from pulling during the machine-appliqué process.

During the actual machine-appliqué process, you will be layering one shape on top of another. Where two fabrics overlap, the underneath piece does not have to be turned under or stitched down.

Thread the top of the machine with thread to match the fabric patches or with threads that coordinate or contrast with fabrics. Rayon thread is a good choice when a sheen is desired on the finished appliqué stitches. Do not use rayon thread in the bobbin; use all-purpose thread.

When all machine work is complete, remove stabilizer from the back referring to the manufacturer's instructions.

Putting It All Together

Finishing the Top
Settings. Most quilts are made by sewing individual blocks together in rows that, when joined, create a design. There are several other methods used to join blocks. Sometimes the setting choice is determined by the block's design. For example, a House block should be placed upright on a quilt, not sideways or upside down.

Plain blocks can be alternated with pieced or appliquéd blocks in a straight set. Making a quilt using plain blocks saves time;

General Instructions

half the number of pieced or appliquéd blocks are needed to make the same-size quilt as shown in Figure 1.

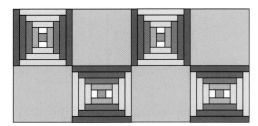

Figure 1
Alternate plain blocks with pieced blocks to save time.

Adding Borders. Borders are an integral part of the quilt and should complement the colors and designs used in the quilt center. Borders frame a quilt just like a mat and frame do a picture.

If fabric strips are added for borders, they may be mitered or butted at the corners as shown in Figures 2 and 3. To determine the size for butted border strips, measure across the center of the completed quilt top from one side raw edge to the other side raw edge. This measurement will include a ¼" seam allowance.

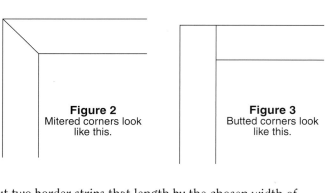

Figure 2
Mitered corners look
like this.

Figure 3
Butted corners look
like this.

Cut two border strips that length by the chosen width of the border. Sew these strips to the top and bottom of the pieced center referring to Figure 4. Press the seam allowance toward the border strips.

Measure across the completed quilt top at the center, from top raw edge to bottom raw edge, including the two border strips

already added. Cut two border strips that length by the chosen width of the border. Sew a strip to each of the two remaining sides as shown in Figure 4. Press the seams toward the border strips.

Figure 4
Sew border strips to
opposite sides; sew
remaining 2 strips to
remaining sides to make
butted corners.

To make mitered corners, measure the quilt as before. To this add twice the width of the border and ½" for seam allowances to determine the length of the strips. Repeat for opposite sides. Sew on each strip, stopping stitching ¼" from corner, leaving the remainder of the strip dangling.

Press corners at a 45-degree angle to form a crease. Stitch from the inside quilt corner to the outside on the creased line. Trim excess away after stitching and press mitered seams open (Figures 5–7).

Carefully press the entire piece, including the pieced center. Avoid pulling and stretching while pressing, which would distort shapes.

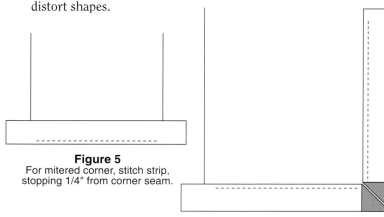

Figure 5
For mitered corner, stitch strip,
stopping 1/4" from corner seam.

Figure 6
Fold and press corner to make a
45-degree angle.

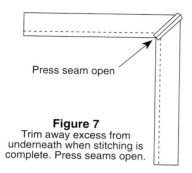

Figure 7
Trim away excess from underneath when stitching is complete. Press seams open.

Getting Ready to Quilt

Choosing a Quilting Design. If you choose to hand- or machine-quilt your finished top, you will need to select a design for quilting.

There are several types of quilting designs, some of which may not have to be marked. The easiest of the unmarked designs is in-the-ditch quilting. Here the quilting stitches are placed in the valley created by the seams joining two pieces together or next to the edge of an appliqué design. There is no need to mark a top for in-the-ditch quilting. Machine quilters choose this option because the stitches are not as obvious on the finished quilt. (Figure 8).

Outline-quilting ¼" or more away from seams or appliqué shapes is another no-mark alternative (Figure 9) that prevents having to sew through the layers made by seams, thus making stitching easier.

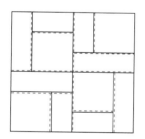

Figure 8
In-the-ditch quilting is done in the seam that joins 2 pieces.

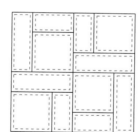

Figure 9
Outline-quilting 1/4" away from seam is a popular choice for quilting.

If you are not comfortable eyeballing the ¼" (or other distance), masking tape is available in different widths and is helpful to place on straight-edge designs to mark the quilting line. If using masking tape, place the tape right up against the seam and quilt close to the other edge.

Meander or free-motion quilting by machine fills in open spaces and doesn't require marking. It is fun and easy to stitch as shown in Figure 10.

Marking the Top for Quilting. If you choose a fancy or allover design for quilting, you will need to transfer the design to your quilt top before layering with the backing and batting. You may use a sharp medium-lead or silver pencil on light background fabrics. Test the pencil marks to guarantee that they will wash out of your quilt top when quilting is complete; or be sure your quilting stitches cover the pencil marks. Mechanical pencils with very fine points may be used successfully to mark quilts.

Figure 10
Machine meander quilting fills in large spaces.

Manufactured quilt-design templates are available in many designs and sizes and are cut out of a durable plastic template material that is easy to use.

To make a permanent quilt-design template, choose a template material on which to transfer the design. See-through plastic is the best as it will let you place the design while allowing you to see where it is in relation to your quilt design without moving it. Place the design on the quilt top where you want it and trace around it with your marking tool. Pick up the quilting template and place again; repeat marking.

No matter what marking method you use, remember—the marked lines should never show on the finished quilt. When the top is marked, it is ready for layering.

Preparing the Quilt Backing. The quilt backing is a very important feature of your quilt. The materials listed for each quilt in this book includes the size requirements for the backing, not the yardage needed. Exceptions to this are when the backing fabric is also used on the quilt top and yardage is given for that fabric.

A backing is generally cut at least 4" larger than the quilt top or 2" larger on all sides. For a 64" x 78" finished quilt, the backing would need to be at least 68" x 82".

To avoid having the seam across the center of the quilt

General Instructions

backing, cut or tear one of the right-length pieces in half and sew half to each side of the second piece as shown in Figure 11.

Quilts that need a backing more than 88" wide may be pieced in horizontal pieces as shown in Figure 12.

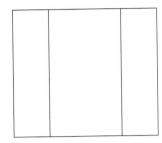

Figure 11
Center 1 backing piece with a piece on each side.

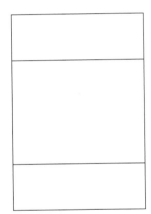

Figure 12
Horizontal seams may be used on backing pieces.

Layering the Quilt Sandwich. Layering the quilt top with the batting and backing is time-consuming. Open the batting several days before you need it and place over a bed or flat on the floor to help flatten the creases caused from its being folded up in the bag for so long.

Iron the backing piece, folding in half both vertically and horizontally and pressing to mark centers.

If you will not be quilting on a frame, place the backing right side down on a clean floor or table. Start in the center and push any wrinkles or bunches flat. Use masking tape to tape the edges to the floor or large clips to hold the backing to the

edges of the table. The backing should be taut.

Place the batting on top of the backing, matching centers using fold lines as guides; flatten out any wrinkles. Trim the batting to the same size as the backing.

Fold the quilt top in half lengthwise and place on top of the batting, wrong side against the batting, matching centers. Unfold quilt and, working from the center to the outside edges, smooth out any wrinkles or lumps.

To hold the quilt layers together for quilting, baste by hand or use safety pins. If basting by hand, thread a long thin needle with a long piece of unknotted white or off-white thread. Starting in the center and leaving a long tail, make 4"–6" stitches toward the outside edge of the quilt top, smoothing as you baste. Start at the center again and work toward the outside as shown in Figure 13.

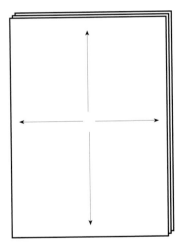

Figure 13
Baste from the center to the outside edges.

If quilting by machine, you may prefer to use safety pins for holding your fabric sandwich together. Start in the center of the quilt and pin to the outside, leaving pins open until all are placed. When you are satisfied that all layers are smooth, close the pins.

Quilting

Hand Quilting. Hand quilting is the process of placing stitches through the quilt top, batting and backing to hold them together. While it is a functional process, it also adds beauty and loft to the finished quilt.

To begin, thread a sharp between needle with an 18" piece of quilting thread. Tie a small knot in the end of the thread. Position the needle about ½" to 1" away from the starting point on quilt top. Sink the needle through the top into the batting layer but not through the backing. Pull the needle up at the starting point of the quilting design. Pull the needle and thread until the knot sinks through the top into the batting (Figure 14).

Some stitchers like to take a backstitch here at the beginning while others prefer to begin the first stitch here. Take small, even running stitches along the marked quilting line (Figure 15). Keep one hand positioned underneath to feel the needle go all the way through to the backing.

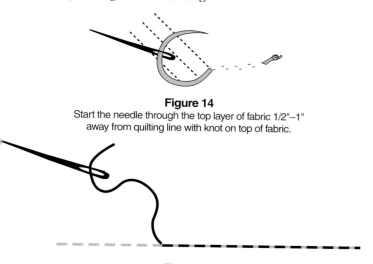

Figure 14
Start the needle through the top layer of fabric 1/2"–1" away from quilting line with knot on top of fabric.

Figure 15
Make small, even running stitches on marked quilting line.

When you have nearly run out of thread, wind the thread around the needle several times to make a small knot and pull it close to the fabric. Insert the needle into the fabric on the quilting line and come out with the needle ½" to 1" away, pulling the knot into the fabric layers the same as when you started. Pull and cut thread close to fabric. The end should disappear inside after cutting. Some quilters prefer to take a backstitch with a loop through it for a knot to end.

Machine Quilting. Successful machine quilting requires practice and a good relationship with your sewing machine.

Prepare the quilt for machine quilting in the same way as for hand quilting. Use safety pins to hold the layers together instead of basting with thread.

Presser-foot quilting is best used for straight-line quilting because the presser bar lever does not need to be continually lifted.

Set the machine on a longer stitch length (3.0 or 8–10 stitches to the inch). Too tight a stitch causes puckering and fabric tucks, either on the quilt top or backing. An even-feed or walking foot helps to eliminate the tucks and puckering by feeding the upper and lower layers through the machine evenly. Before you begin, loosen the amount of pressure on the presser foot.

Special machine-quilting needles work best to penetrate the three layers in your quilt.

Decide on a design. Quilting in the ditch is not quite as visible, but if you quilt with the feed dogs engaged, it means turning the quilt frequently. It is not easy to fit a rolled-up quilt through the small opening on the sewing machine head.

Meander quilting is the easiest way to machine-quilt—and it is fun. Meander quilting is done using an appliqué or darning foot with the feed dogs dropped. It is sort of like scribbling. Simply move the quilt top around under the foot and make stitches in a random pattern to fill the space. The same method may be used to outline a quilt design. The trick is the same as in hand quilting; you are striving for stitches of uniform size. Your hands are in complete control of the design.

If machine quilting is of interest to you, there are several very good books available at quilt shops that will help you become a successful machine quilter.

Finishing the Edges

After your quilt is tied or quilted, the edges need to be finished. Decide how you want the edges of your quilt finished before layering the backing and batting with the quilt top.

Without Binding—Self-Finish. There is one way to eliminate adding an edge finish. This is done before quilting. Place the batting on a flat surface. Place the pieced top right side up on the batting. Place the backing right sides together with the pieced top. Pin and/or baste the layers together to hold flat referring to Layering the Quilt Sandwich.

General Instructions

Begin stitching in the center of one side using a ¼" seam allowance, reversing at the beginning and end of the seam. Continue stitching all around and back to the beginning side. Leave a 12" or larger opening. Clip corners to reduce excess. Turn right side out through the opening. Slipstitch the opening closed by hand. The quilt may now be quilted by hand or machine.

The disadvantage to this method is that once the edges are sewn in, any creases or wrinkles that might form during the quilting process cannot be flattened out. Tying is the preferred method for finishing a quilt constructed using this method.

Bringing the backing fabric to the front is another way to finish the quilt's edge without binding. To accomplish this, complete the quilt as for hand or machine quilting. Trim the batting only even with the front. Trim the backing 1" larger than the completed top all around.

Turn the backing edge in ½" and then turn over to the front along edge of batting. The folded edge may be machine-stitched close to the edge through all layers, or blind-stitched in place to finish.

The front may be turned to the back. If using this method, a wider front border is needed. The backing and batting are trimmed 1" smaller than the top and the top edge is turned under ½" and then turned to the back and stitched in place.

One more method of self-finish may be used. The top and backing may be stitched together by hand at the edge. To accomplish this, all quilting must be stopped ½" from the quilt-top edge. The top and backing of the quilt are trimmed even and the batting is trimmed to ¼"–½" smaller. The edges of the top and backing are turned in ¼"–½" and blind-stitched together at the very edge.

These methods do not require the use of extra fabric and save time in preparation of binding strips; they are not as durable as an added binding.

Binding. The technique of adding extra fabric at the edges of the quilt is called binding. The binding encloses the edges and adds an extra layer of fabric for durability.

To prepare the quilt for the addition of the binding, trim the batting and backing layers flush with the top of the quilt using a rotary cutter and ruler or shears. Using a walking-foot attachment (sometimes called an even-feed foot attachment), machine-baste the three layers together all around approximately ⅛" from the cut edge.

The materials listed for each quilt in this book often includes a number of yards of self-made or purchased binding. Bias binding may be purchased in packages and in many colors. The advantage to self-made binding is that you can use fabrics from your quilt to coordinate colors. Double-fold, straight-grain binding and double-fold, bias-grain binding are two of the most commonly used types of binding.

Double-fold, straight-grain binding is used on smaller projects with right-angle corners. Double-fold, bias-grain binding is best suited for bed-size quilts or quilts with rounded corners.

To make double-fold, straight-grain binding, cut 2¼"-wide strips of fabric across the width or down the length of the fabric totaling the perimeter of the quilt plus 10". The strips are joined as shown in Figure 16 and pressed in half wrong sides together along the length using an iron on a cotton setting with no steam.

Figure 16
Join binding strips in a
diagonal seam to eliminate
bulk as shown.

Lining up the raw edges, place the binding on the top of the quilt and begin sewing (again using the walking foot) approximately 6" from the beginning of the binding strip. Stop sewing ¼" from the first corner, leave the needle in the quilt, turn and sew diagonally to the corner as shown in Figure 17.

Fold the binding at a 45-degree angle up and away from the quilt as shown in Figure 18 and back down flush with the raw edges. Starting at the top raw edge of the quilt, begin sewing the next side as shown in Figure 19. Repeat at the next three corners.

As you approach the beginning of the binding strip, stop stitching and overlap the binding ½" from the edge; trim. Join the two ends with a ¼" seam allowance and press the seam open. Reposition the joined binding along the edge of the quilt and resume stitching to the beginning.

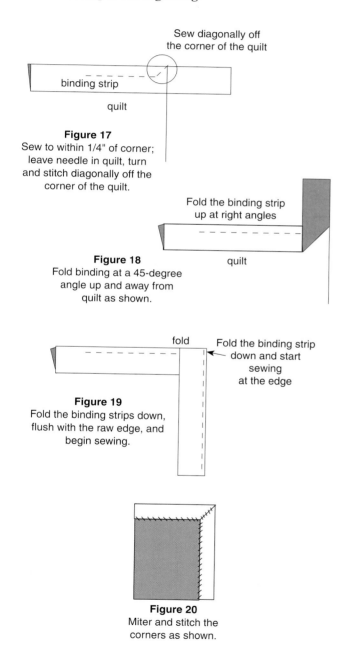

Figure 17
Sew to within 1/4" of corner; leave needle in quilt, turn and stitch diagonally off the corner of the quilt.

Figure 18
Fold binding at a 45-degree angle up and away from quilt as shown.

Figure 19
Fold the binding strips down, flush with the raw edge, and begin sewing.

Figure 20
Miter and stitch the corners as shown.

To finish, bring the folded edge of the binding over the raw edges and blind-stitch the binding in place over the machine-stitching line on the backside. Hand-miter the corners on the back as shown in Figure 20.

If you are making a quilt to be used on a bed, you may want to use double-fold, bias-grain bindings because the many threads that cross each other along the fold at the edge of the quilt make it a more durable binding.

Cut 2¼"-wide bias strips from a large square of fabric. Join the strips as illustrated in Figure 16 and press the seams open. Fold the beginning end of the bias strip ¼" from the raw edge and press. Fold the joined strips in half along the long side, wrong sides together, and press with no steam (Figure 21).

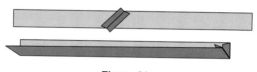

Figure 21
Fold and press strip in half.

Follow the same procedures as previously described for preparing the quilt top and sewing the binding to the quilt top. Treat the corners just as you treated them with straight-grain binding.

Since you are using bias-grain binding, you do have the option to just eliminate the corners if this option doesn't interfere with the patchwork in the quilt. Round the corners off by placing one of your dinner plates at the corner and rotary-cutting the gentle curve (Figure 22).

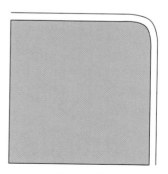

Figure 22
Round corners to eliminate square-corner finishes.

General Instructions

As you approach the beginning of the binding strip, stop stitching and lay the end across the beginning so it will slip inside the fold. Cut the end at a 45-degree angle so the raw edges are contained inside the beginning of the strip (Figure 23). Resume stitching to the beginning. Bring the fold to the back of the quilt and hand-stitch as previously described.

Figure 23
End the binding strips as shown.

Overlapped corners are not quite as easy as rounded ones, but a bit easier than mitering. To make overlapped corners, sew binding strips to opposite sides of the quilt top. Stitch edges down to finish. Trim ends even.

Sew a strip to each remaining side, leaving 1½"–2" excess at each end. Turn quilt over and fold binding down even with previous finished edge as shown in Figure 24.

Figure 24
Fold end of binding even with previous page.

Fold binding in toward quilt and stitch down as before, enclosing the previous bound edge in the seam as shown in Figure 25. It may be necessary to trim the folded-down section to reduce bulk.

Figure 25
An overlapped corner is not quite as neat as a mitered corner.

Final Touches

If your quilt will be hung on the wall, a hanging sleeve is required. Other options include purchased plastic rings or fabric tabs. The best choice is a fabric sleeve, which will evenly distribute the weight of the quilt across the top edge, rather than at selected spots where tabs or rings are stitched, keep the quilt hanging straight and not damage the batting.

To make a sleeve, measure across the top of the finished quilt. Cut an 8"-wide piece of muslin equal to that length—you may need to seam several muslin strips together to make the required length.

Fold in ¼" on each end of the muslin strip and press. Fold again and stitch to hold. Fold the muslin strip lengthwise with right sides together. Sew along the long side to make a tube. Turn the tube right side out; press with seam at bottom or centered on the back.

Hand-stitch the tube along the top of the quilt and the bottom of the tube to the quilt back making sure the quilt lies flat. Stitches should not go through to the front of the quilt and don't need to be too close together as shown in Figure 26.

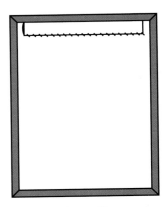

Figure 26
Sew a sleeve to the top back of the quilt.

Slip a wooden dowel or long curtain rod through the sleeve to hang.

When the quilt is finally complete, it should be signed and dated. Use a permanent pen on the back of the quilt. Other methods include cross-stitching your name and date on the front or back or making a permanent label which may be stitched to the back. ❖